WHAT ARE THEY HIDING?

JULIE TIBBOTT

# MEMBER

## Secret Societies, Sects

# S ONLY

## and Cults — Exposed!

# TABLE OF

**Connect with Zest!**

- zestbooks.net/blog
- zestbooks.net/contests
- twitter.com/zestbooks
- facebook.com/zestbook
- facebook.com/BooksWithATwist
- pinterest.com/zestbooks

35 Stillman Street, Suite 121, San Francisco, CA 94107 / www.zestbooks.net

# CONTENTS

Manufactured in the U.S.A.
DOC 10 9 8 7 6 5 4 3 2 1
4500513171

"I refuse to
would have

join any club that
me as a member."

— GROUCHO MARX

Not necessarily the kind of place where you'd
expect to find the masters of the universe.

M.M. MINDERHOUD

# THE BILDERBERG GROUP

FOUNDED: *1954*

STATUS: *Meets once a year.*

EXCLUSIVITY FACTOR: *Very, very, very high — only oligarchs, heads of state, and other ultra-powerful people are allowed access.*

SECRECY FACTOR: *The discussion at their meetings is strictly off the record.*

THREAT FACTOR: *High — it's said that this group is a "shadow government" that runs the world.*

QUIRK FACTOR: *Bilderberg is a magnet for tinfoil hat level conspiracy theorists, who can be found vigorously protesting outside of the conference.*

## HISTORY AND BACKGROUND

We peons often feel like we aren't getting straight talk from the honchos in charge—but there is at least one place where those fat cats can speak frankly about issues that have worldwide repercussions. Bilderberg is an annual conference for about one hundred and forty of the world's most powerful people. The group first met in 1954, with the purpose of shoring up US-European relations and preventing another world war. Now the aim of their annual get-together is to provide a venue for global elites to share ideas about the future of the world. What makes it a little sketchy is that the Bilderbergers don't share the content of their discussions with the people who are affected by their outcomes. What happens at Bilderberg stays at Bilderberg.

So, who are the high rollers in the Bilderberg Group? It's an international crew of royals, presidents, prime ministers, parliamentarians, cabinet members, media magnates, and CEOs of many banks and massive corporations. And while Bilderbergers say that these off-the-record rap sessions simply allow them to deliberate openly on matters of importance, some outsiders suspect that the members are part of something much more sinister than the world's most exclusive debate club.

Conspiracy theorists believe the group is a threat to democracy, bent on organizing an international government—a New World Order. They accuse Bilderbergers of everything from engineering the credit crunch to planning to kill 80 percent of the world population. Conspiracy theorists also think that Bilderbergers representing corporate interests rubbing shoulders with politicians at the conference reeks of lobbying. Members insist that what happens at Bilderberg doesn't affect policy, but we may never know the truth.

## MEMBERSHIP REQUIREMENTS

You have to be pretty darn influential to be asked to join the Bilderberg Group. If you aren't an aristocrat, a powerful politician, the CEO of a major corporation, or some other global leader, you've got no chance of getting in. The gathering is invite-only, and the guest list changes from year to year. Past attendees include former US president Bill Clinton, founder and CEO of Amazon.com Jeff Bezos, and ex-CIA director David Petraeus.

## INSIDE THE BILDERBERG GROUP

The group's first meeting took place at the Hotel de Bilderberg, located in Oosterbeek in the Netherlands. Since then, the annual gathering has been held at luxury hotels all over the world. The conference lasts four days, and attendees are required to stay for the entire duration. As they arrive in their private helicopters and chauffeured limos, they are greeted by protesters bearing signs that say things like: "STOP NEW WORLD ORDER" and

"OLIGARCHS, THE SPAWN OF SATAN." The location, guest list, and agenda for the meeting used to be totally classified. That information is released to the public now, but it's still a far cry from transparency. Inside their highly secured location, Bilderbergers discuss topics such as nuclear power, cyber warfare, job creation, and the US presidency (which they've been accused of fixing). The minutes of the meeting are never released. After the secret summit, the Bilderbergers return to their lairs, leaving the rest of us to wonder how the decisions made at Bilderberg might affect our world. ▲

# ELITE RETREATS

Despite the cushy accommodations, Bilderberg doesn't seem like much of a vacation. So where do the fat cats go for fun? These are a few of the most exclusive spots.

## BOHEMIAN GROVE

If a Rockefeller pees in the woods and there's no one around to hear it, does it make a sound? You can only find out in the wilds of Bohemian Grove, a campground in the midst of a California redwood forest where some of the most powerful men in the world gather every summer for a three-week retreat.

The Grove is property of a San Francisco-based men's club established in 1782. Some "Boho" hopefuls may have been on the absurdly long waiting list since that time. But those lucky enough to score an invite to the camp might bunk with politicians, CEOs, military contractors, and other influential men. Richard Nixon—along with many other US presidents—has visited the woods, as has newscaster Walter Cronkite, and even singer Jimmy Buffett. (And yes, they actually do stay in bunks.)

Just like at any other sleep-away camp, the campers form strong bonds over activities such as bird watching, dominoes, and campfire sing-alongs (hopefully not to Jimmy Buffett songs). Unlike a camp for kids though, all festivities at the Grove are fueled by large amounts of alcohol, which is mandatory to consume. But the "Grovers" do indulge in some rather childish hijinks during their stay, including the aforementioned public urination, and hamming it up in the Grove's annual musical comedy. Whether or not they make lanyards is unknown.

Smokey the Bear and the California Forest Service probably wouldn't appreciate all the cigar smoking that goes on among the old growth redwood trees, but there's another Grove tradition that could easily cause a forest fire: The Cremation of Care. This opening ceremony entails the crypt of "Mr. Dull Care" being torched and set adrift on a lake, followed by fireworks.

This ritual is meant to symbolize letting go of outside cares and worries, which is the purpose of a stay at Bohemian Grove.

## CAMP DAVID

Being rulers of the free world has its perks. One of them is access to Camp David, the country home of the President of the United States. Every president since Franklin D. Roosevelt has made use of the place, located about sixty miles outside of Washington, DC, in the wooded hills of Catoctin Mountain Park near Thurmont, Maryland. Formally known as Naval Support Facility Thurmont, military personnel provide staffing and security and take good care keeping intruders away from the very private property.

The retreat was established in 1942, when FDR was in need of a place to escape the oppressively muggy DC summers. With its cool mountain air, beautiful grounds, and close proximity to the capitol, this secluded spot fit the bill. FDR called it "Shangri-La" after the idyllic mountain kingdom in James Hilton's book *Lost Horizon*. In 1953, President Dwight Eisenhower

Best dressed: JFK. (Second Best: The Secret Service agent behind JFK?)

renamed it "Camp David" in honor of his grandson. Little David and plenty of other presidential family members after him have enjoyed the camp's many amenities, including a pool, putting green, driving range, tennis courts, and gym.

In addition to recreation, Camp David has also been the site of many historic meetings. The presidents have hosted a number of foreign dignitaries there over the years. In the informal setting, FDR and British Prime Minister Winston Churchill planned the Allies' invasion of Europe during WWII. In 1978, President Jimmy Carter held top-secret negotiations with Middle Eastern leaders there, resulting in the peace treaty between Israel and Egypt known as the Camp David Accords. More recently, President Barack Obama chose the site to host the 2012 G8 Summit.

Running the country is surely a stressful job, but when the president needs a break from the White House, the tranquility of Camp David is only a half-hour helicopter ride away.

## AUGUSTA NATIONAL GOLF CLUB

It's another boys' club—well, an old men's club, really. The average age of the members at this most rarified of country clubs located in Augusta, Georgia, is over seventy. That probably explains why these stodgy, stuck-in-their-ways oldsters refused to admit women to their club until 2012, when they reluctantly opened the doors to just two ladies, one of them being former Secretary of State Condoleezza Rice. And they didn't admit black members until 1990. One of the founders had once haughtily declared, "As long as I'm alive, all the golfers will be white and all the caddies will be black."

So why would anybody feel honored to be part of such a racist, sexist institution? Because when it comes to golf, Augusta National is the gold standard. Founded in 1933 on the site of an old indigo plantation, the club hosts the Masters tournament and is considered the best course in America. Augusta National's once-confidential membership list —first revealed to the public in 2004—is packed with statesmen, politicians, and major corporate leaders. Bill Gates, Warren Buffett, and T. Boone Pickens are just a few of the

*One of the few places where arranging a flyover is more affordable than simply walking in.*

high rollers on the roster. Golf has always been about wheeling and dealing with cronies on the course just as much as actually playing the game, so these honchos are able to form some high-level alliances out on the links.

Every one of the three hundred or so members gets a green jacket upon joining up, but those blazers don't come cheap. Membership fees are about $10,000 per year. However, simply being willing to cough up lots of cash doesn't get one the privilege of kicking back in this clubhouse. You can't apply to join Augusta National—it's invite-only. Over-eager hopefuls who make it known they want in are shunned. As a sport, golf may be becoming more diverse and inclusive, but the Augusta National Golf Club remains a highly elite institution frozen in time. ▲

Scary dolls convention.

# THE BIZANGO

FOUNDED: *18th century, when the French brought thousands of slaves from Africa to Haiti.*

STATUS: *Still active in rural Haiti, where a belief in zombies persists.*

EXCLUSIVITY FACTOR: *Inclusion is by invitation only, and members must have some knowledge of sorcery.*

SECRECY FACTOR: *It is said that members will die before they will tell the secrets of the Bizango, and those who dare speak about it are punished severely.*

THREAT FACTOR: *High. The Bizango is responsible for policing many rural areas of Haiti, and peasants are reportedly afraid to speak out against this powerful group for fear they will be turned into zombies.*

QUIRK FACTOR: *The Voodoo religion has been widely spoofed, with caricatures of witch doctors, voodoo dolls, and the like. However, Bizango practices are different from regular Voodoo worship.*

## HISTORY AND BACKGROUND

Those who live in fear of the zombie apocalypse best stay out of Haiti. Many believe that this Caribbean country is home to the living dead—people turned into zombies by "magical" means and then forced into slavery.

According to legend (a phrase which should be borne in mind throughout this section), secret societies, collectively known as the Bizango, rule the Haitian countryside. The societies are a legacy of colonial Haiti—composed of modern-day descendants of escaped slaves. They maintain law and order in their communities and dole out justice to wrongdoers. The most horrible punishment they have in their repertoire is zombification—with the fear of such a fate keeping locals from crossing this powerful secret society.

Zombies feature prominently is Haitian folklore. Unlike the terrified folks in Hollywood horror movies who want to defeat the undead, Haitians aren't afraid *of* zombies—sometimes, if rescued, a zombified person will actually be taken in and cared for by relatives. Rather, Haitians are scared of *becoming* zombies—a fear that echoes the days of slavery, when they were helpless to defy their white masters.

So how does one become a zombie? The first step is "dying." There exists a "zombie powder," the main psychoactive ingredient of which is Tetrodotoxin, a toxin derived from a puffer fish found in Haitian waters. Additional ingredients are said to be tarantulas and other sea creatures. This powder is transferred to the victim via an open wound, and when the poison gets into the bloodstream, the victim falls ill and "dies" within a matter of hours. . . Except the victim is not truly dead but in a temporary coma-like state of paralysis mimicking death that even doctors have mistaken for the real thing.

In rural Haiti, dead bodies (as well as those believed to be dead) are not embalmed; moreover they are often interred in aboveground crypts—practices that make capturing and creating a zombie easier than they would be in other parts of the world. Some families of the deceased, if they are unsure whether their relative is truly dead, take precautions against this by keeping watch in the cemetery for several days to deter grave robbers. Another solution is cutting open or poisoning bodies to ensure real death. There is also a more Indiana Jones-style method of protecting against crypt creepers: A knife is placed in the right hand of the corpse, and the arm is flexed in such a way that it will spring up to stab whoever disturbs the body.

But if a Bizango zombie-maker or his assistants manage to abscond with a living body, they will wait until the person regains consciousness to administer another drug, a hallucinogen that keeps the victim docile. Then, the "zombie" is often sold to a master and forced to toil on the sugar plantations that still survive on the island. For residents of a country that fought so dearly for freedom from their French oppressors, a life of servitude as a zombie is the ultimate torture.

# MEMBERSHIP REQUIREMENTS

No amateur zombie masters need apply: to join the Bizango, one must have some knowledge of sorcery. Prominent figures such as Voodoo priests, chefs de section (local magistrates), and other elected officials may take part, thus strengthening the group's authority. Membership is voluntary but exclusive—candidates must be invited to join. If an individual is found to be an acceptable candidate, he or she must agree to contribute financially to the group, to respect the hierarchy, and, most importantly, to uphold the secrecy of their magical rituals. Both men and women can hold seats in the complicated hierarchy of the group, which includes positions such as emperor, flag queen, and prefect of discipline. One's ranking is revealed through subtle manipulation of the fingers while shaking hands to greet another member.

After a candidate masters the secret handshake and other cryptic forms of Bizango communication and proves his or her loyalty, the president of the society may decide to accept the candidate as a permanent member. The induction ceremony requires the initiate to ingest two potions: one bitter and one sweet, embodying the Bizango motto "Sweet as honey, bitter as bile." Sweet, because the society is good to deserving parties; and bitter, because members must enforce the rules by means that are surely *not* sweet. The initiate then swears before the society on pain of death not to reveal their secrets and ingests yet another potion—this one much harsher on the system, said to "leave the clothes on your back in shreds." It's also alleged that some members receive a tattoo to protect them from black magic spells, though some of the Bizango themselves are in fact bokors, or practitioners of black magic.

# INSIDE THE BIZANGO

Another Bizango motto is "Order and respect for the night," and that is reflected in their nocturnal meetings. One fairly recent account has the Bizango members dressed in red and black robes, meeting in a makeshift temple decorated with images of sinister spirits. The temple is lit by a candle perched on a human skull. (Other centuries-old Bizango art incorporating human skulls has been found, so this morbid detail rings true.)

The robed attendants then dance and sing, praising Voodoo gods called loa. Next, they fall into an ordered line according to Bizango rank and pay their respects to a small black coffin, offering money and other sacrifices. Drumming, dancing, and singing continue on through the night, an indication to others in the village to stay inside so as not to disturb the festivities.

It's not a party that most villagers wish to attend. If someone dares cross either a member of the society or another person in the community, they can be brought before the Bizango for a trial. A man named Clairvius Narcisse was one such offender. In 1962, he was zombified by the Bizango on account of his failure to support his illegitimate children. A doctor signed his death certificate—but eighteen years later, Narcisse showed up in his home village, very much alive.

Narcisse told the horrible story of the years he spent in zombie servitude. He was given the zombie powder and subsequently "died." While others gathered round his deathbed, he was completely cognizant but unable to express this to anyone. Then, to his horror, he was buried alive. Less than twenty-four hours later, Narcisse was removed from his grave by a bokor and his assistants, who beat him violently. Traumatized, Narcisse was then given another drug that possibly helped to erase his memory and keep him subservient. The zombie makers then led him to labor in the fields on a remote part of the island where he would not be recognized.

Continued doses of the drug kept Narcisse docile and passive for years— but when his zombie master died and could no longer administer the toxin, its effect eventually wore off, and Narcisse wandered back home. He had a scar on his cheek, said to be from a nail driven into his coffin.

Creating and transporting zombies is serious business for the Bizango. They are authorized to issue a paper called a laissez-passer, and seizing a zombie is illegal without an official transfer of the document. Their control over the zombie population is what keeps the communities they preside over obedient. If someone dares go to higher authorities with accusations against the

Bizango, the charges may not be pursued—and for the accuser, there may be hell to pay. Even some more educated, urban Haitians are reluctant to meddle in the society's affairs for fear of being turned into zombies themselves.

And for Bizango members who break the code of secrecy, there is severe punishment in store. Death (real death) seems preferable to this terrifying scenario: In one society, wrongdoers are taken out in a boat and, when far from land, are beaten and poisoned with the zombie potion. While still conscious, the traitor is pushed overboard, knowing that once the poison sets in, he'll be helpless and unable to swim to shore.

And for Bizango members who break the code of secrecy, there is severe punishment in store. In one society, wrongdoers are taken out in a boat and, when far from land, are beaten and poisoned with the zombie potion. While still conscious, the traitor is pushed overboard, knowing that once the poison sets in, he'll be helpless and unable to swim to shore. Death (real death) seems preferable to this terrifying scenario—even if it is just another part of the Bizango myth. ▲

# SMILE, YOU'RE ON UNDEAD CAMERA!

There have been dozens of films, TV shows, and video games about zombies—the fake Hollywood kind. But it was author Zora Neale Hurston who was reportedly the first person to catch a real Haitian zombie on film. In the 1920s, Hurston was at the center of the Harlem Renaissance, and became most famous for her novel *Their Eyes Were Watching God*. Hurston also undertook anthropological work, traveling to Jamaica and Haiti in the mid-1930s to observe the culture and Voodoo practices. In her book *Tell My Horse*, she recorded what little firsthand ethnography of zombies is available to this day.

In Haiti, Hurston heard many chilling accounts of zombies, and experienced for herself the fear of these creatures that permeated the culture. Wary Haitians warned Hurston against associating with zombies and their makers, but the curious author persisted. A zombified woman had been taken to a hospital, where Hurston took her famous photo. Hurston said:

> I had the rare opportunity to see and touch an authentic case. I listened to the broken noises in its throat, and then, I did what no one else had ever done, I photographed it. . . . I took her first in the position that she assumed herself whenever left alone. That is, cringing against the wall with the cloth hiding her face and head. Then in other positions. Finally the doctor forcibly uncovered her and held her so that I could take her face. And the sight was dreadful. That blank face with the dead eyes. The eyelids were white all around the eyes as if they had been burned with acid. It was pronounced enough to come out in the picture. There was nothing that you could say to her or get from her except by looking at her, and the sight of this wreckage was too much to endure for long.

The woman's name was Felicia Felix-Mentor, and records show she died and was buried in 1907. Then, in 1936, she was found wandering naked to a farm where she had once lived. Her brother recognized her as his sister who died 29 years earlier. Though the zombie woman's state was surely drug-induced, Hurston was shaken by the encounter:

> *If I had not experienced all of this in the strong sunlight of a hospital yard, I might have come away from Haiti interested but doubtful. But I saw this case of Felicia Felix-Mentor, which was vouched for by the highest authority. So I know that there are zombies in Haiti.* ▲

Carl Van Vechten's iconic portrait of Zora Neale Hurston.

# GHOULS ON FILM

The zombies in the movies aren't nearly as scary as the real-life victims of the Bizango—and are much more entertaining. Check out these fearsome flicks.

## WHITE ZOMBIE, 1932

Considered the first film of the zombie genre, Béla Lugosi stars as a nefarious Voodoo priest who turns an innocent young woman into a zombie.

## I WALKED WITH A ZOMBIE, 1943

A young nurse is summoned to a Caribbean island to care for a plantation owner's ailing wife, who she suspects might be a zombie.

## NIGHT OF THE LIVING DEAD, 1968

In this classic of the genre, reanimated corpses leave their graves and attack an isolated farmhouse in search of human flesh.

## THE SERPENT AND THE RAINBOW, 1988

One of the few zombie movies that take place in Haiti, this film is loosely based on the nonfiction book of the same name by ethnobotanist Wade Davis.

## ARMY OF DARKNESS, 1992

In this horror comedy, a time-traveling hero battles Dark Age zombies called "deadites."

## DEAD ALIVE, 1992

Rat-monkey hybrids carry a deadly virus that turns people into zombies in this gory cult classic.

## 28 DAYS LATER, 2002

A highly contagious virus sweeps through the world, leaving most of the population zombified—and four British survivors must battle their way to safety.

## DAWN OF THE DEAD, 2004

This remake of George Romero's 1978 film of the same name is full of scares as fast-moving zombies take over a shopping mall.

## SHAUN OF THE DEAD, 2004

In this zombie comedy, a doltish Londoner must rise to the occasion and fight when the living dead take over his town.

## I AM LEGEND, 2007

In a zombie-ridden New York City, a virologist played by Will Smith scrambles to find an antidote to their virus, with only his dog for company.

## ZOMBIELAND, 2009

Teens go on a gleeful zombie-killing road trip that's far more fun than it is scary. ▲

"Care to join us...?"

FROM WHITE ZOMBIE

The truly grisly scene at the Branch
Davidian compound in Waco in 1993.

# BRANCH DAVIDIANS

FOUNDED: *1955; although leadership was taken over by David Koresh in 1990.*

STATUS: *They still exist today, going by the name Branch, The Lord Our Righteousness.*

EXCLUSIVITY FACTOR: *Only the most radical believers of the Seventh-Day Adventist religion can be a part of this sect.*

SECRECY FACTOR: *When the Branch Davidians were based in a compound in Waco, Texas, any illegal activities were hidden from the outside world.*

THREAT FACTOR: *Debatable—though the Davidians were suspected of stockpiling illegal weapons, and used them to fight back during an FBI siege of their compound in 1993, some say the government took excessive force against the group. It is clear, however, that young girls and women who lived in the compound were under threat of being victims of sexual assault by their leader, David Koresh.*

QUIRK FACTOR: *The Branch Davidians made Waco, Texas, forever synonymous with "The Wacko from Waco," and the horrible tragedy that happened there.*

## HISTORY AND BACKGROUND

Long before David Koresh was known as "The Wacko from Waco," a charismatic leader of a religious sect known as the Branch Davidians, he was a guy named Vernon Wayne Howell, a high school dropout who played a mean guitar and had an extraordinary mastery of scripture.

Even prior to the infamous 1993 raid at the Branch Davidian compound that ended in fire and bloodshed, the group had been through lots of drama already. The Branch Davidians originated from a schism from the Seventh-Day Adventist Church in 1955. Adventists ascribe fiercely to the Bible, believing the scripture to be infallible. As such, they prepare for a day of judgment and the second coming of Christ, as prophesized in the Book of Revelation. The group was based in a rural area outside of Waco, Texas, in the Mount Carmel Center (named after the Biblical Mount Carmel).

When 19-year-old Koresh, originally from Houston, joined the Branch Davidians in 1982, he wasted no time in bidding for leadership of the sect, claiming he had a gift for prophecy. He started a sexual relationship with then-leader of the group, Lois Roden, saying that God wanted him to father a child with a 77-year-old woman. Not surprisingly, Roden never did become impregnated with the Chosen One, as promised by Koresh. The presence of this upstart rankled Lois's son George Roden, who intended to inherit the mantle of leadership from his mother. He exiled Koresh from Mount Carmel in 1984.

It's a testament to the power of Koresh's preaching that some Branch Davidians were inspired to follow him all the way to Palestine—Palestine, Texas, that is. There, the group lived in crude plywood huts and tents, but they remained fiercely devoted to their leader, who eventually captured the loyalty of most of the Branch Davidian community. When Lois Roden died 1986, they hoped to return to Mount Carmel.

George Roden was in charge at the compound in Mount Carmel then, but his influence was rapidly declining. He wanted to debunk this hippie "prophet" who was taking over his church, so in 1987 he came up with a plan he hoped would oust Koresh once and for all. Roden exhumed the body of another Davidian named Anna Hughes from the cemetery at Mount Carmel, and stored the casket inside a shed. He then invited Koresh to have a go at bringing the dead woman back to life. Whichever one of them could manage such a miracle would prove himself as the true prophet.

This request for a resurrection showdown was too outlandish even for Koresh. Instead, he called Roden's bluff and asked the local sheriff's department to arrest Roden for corpse abuse. The officials demanded evidence, so Koresh and seven other men snuck into the compound to photograph the body. They were armed not only with a camera but also with assault rifles, and a shootout ensued. Deputies broke up the melee before anyone was harmed, but Koresh and his accomplices were charged with the attempted murder of George Roden. The jury couldn't reach a verdict on Koresh, and the charges were dropped. Roden, on the other hand, was sentenced to six months in jail on a contempt of court charge. The unhappy prisoner asked God to inflict AIDS and herpes on the Texas Supreme Court judge responsible for releasing Koresh.

Koresh and his followers moved back to Mount Carmel, triumphant. Koresh led the group in marathon Bible study sessions, sometimes lasting up to fifteen hours. He assured them that he was the only one who could open the Seven Seals, an apocalyptic document described in the Bible that would unleash cataclysmic events and bring about the end of the world. The language involving the figurative seals was convoluted and perplexing though, and in the eyes of his acolytes, they needed Koresh to make sense of it. In the Bible, it says that the only one worthy to open the seals is the "Lion of Judah," a phrase used to describe Jesus in the Book of Revelation. Koresh's astrological sign happened to be Leo (the lion), and he used this rather flimsy fact to further bolster his claim to the title of messiah.

But in between all the Bible study, there was some levity in the compound. Unlike the original Jesus, Koresh was no goody-two-shoes. He insisted that Christ was sinful, just like any other man. And boy, could Koresh sin with the best of them. He cursed, drank alcohol, and lusted after women (not to mention that whole attempted murder thing). He had a rock 'n' roll band, through which he hoped to spread his teachings and transform the Seventh-Day Adventist church. He legally changed his name from Vernon Wayne Howell to David Koresh in 1990 to enhance his "music career," but his band of holy-roller rockers never made it on the charts.

But Koresh's other diversions were more troubling. He preached that, as the messiah, he was entitled to have sex with all of the women in the sect, even those who were married. He annulled all of his followers' marriages in 1989, ordering the men to remain celibate while he enjoyed unlimited sexual partners. These partners even included underage girls, like his wife's 12-year-old sister. Koresh's legal wife was 14 years old when he married her (he was 24), but he had over a dozen other so-called "wives," many of whom bore his children. What's more, he is also said to have physically abused these children, whipping an 8-month-old baby and forcing his 3-year-old son to sleep in a rat-infested garage. Disillusioned ex-members of the Branch Davidians who no longer believed Koresh was Christ brought these allegations to light, but there was little authorities could do as long as the victimized cult members remained in their heavily armed compound.

However, the Bureau of Alcohol, Tobacco, and Firearms (ATF) had been keeping tabs on the Branch Davidians, and wanted to raid the compound to recover their stash of weapons. Koresh and his crew were suspected of modifying legal guns to make illegal, automatic firearms. On February 28, 1993, the ATF executed a search warrant of the compound. It did not go smoothly. The Branch Davidians were armed and ready to defend their territory. The result was a 51-day standoff with the ATF, FBI, and Texas National Guard, ending with Mount Carmel engulfed in flames and seventy-six Branch Davidians, including David Koresh, dead.

# MEMBERSHIP REQUIREMENTS

First and foremost, members of Koresh's crew had to be devoted Seventh-Day Adventists. The Adventists are a conservative, fundamentalist Christian sect. They believe in the infallibility of the Scripture and the second coming of Christ. Unlike some other forms of Christianity, the religion of Seventh-Day Adventists allows for end-time prophets, so when someone like David Koresh comes along, they willingly hear him out. Koresh's word spread and attracted followers from Australia, New Zealand, Canada, England, and throughout the United States, many of whom came to live with him at Mount Carmel.

But what drove these people—many of them educated professionals—to trust in the teachings of an abusive pedophile with a ninth-grade education? Former followers say that Koresh's preaching had a thrilling, drug-like effect, and his promise that only he could open the mythical Seven Seals and pave the way to salvation was extremely compelling to those who believed the end was nigh.

There was precedent in their religion when it came to apocalyptic predictions. The Seventh-Day Adventist church has its origins in the teachings of William Miller, a Baptist preacher who claimed the world would end in 1843 and Jesus Christ would return to bring his followers, called Millerites, to heaven. A period called "The Great Disappointment" resulted when that failed to occur, but Millerites did not stop hoping for the second coming of Christ. David Koresh was charismatic and manipulative enough to convince Branch Davidians that he was the savior they were waiting for.

Considering that he raped and abused children and interfered with marriages, it's pretty amazing that Koresh kept so many loyal followers. Simply put, these people were true believers, and they bought the lines that were fed to them by the silver-tongued Koresh—though some may have stayed because they were too ashamed to admit to the world all the lies and indignities they were subjected to by their leader. In lieu of their wives, Koresh promised the men perfect mates in heaven, much more immaculate than the women they were stuck with on earth. As for the women, Koresh said God wanted grandchildren, and the offspring the women of the cult produced with him would rule the world. The women considered it an honor to be chosen by the man they saw as Christ. Koresh groomed even the youngest girls to strive to be part of his harem. The ones targeted for his affections wore necklaces with a six-pointed Star of David pendant.

Sadly, people have always twisted religion to achieve their own ends, and David Koresh's personal desires always seemed to be conveniently sanctioned by God. His most fervent followers would die for supporting his beliefs.

# INSIDE MOUNT CARMEL

The compound at Mount Carmel was only a humble scattering of shacks until Koresh took over and transformed it into a sprawling structure of several floors that included a chapel, residence, gymnasium, water and watch towers, tornado shelter, and swimming pool. The ATF wished to enter to execute an arrest warrant for David Koresh and a search warrant for the facility, but they were wary of the heavily armed guards that were said to patrol the place.

One of their agents had "infiltrated" the Branch Davidians, but unbeknownst to the ATF, the group was aware that the agent was a plant. On the morning of February 28, 1993, the infiltrator entered the compound for Bible study, but left quickly after Koresh confessed to him that he knew a raid was imminent, saying: "Neither the ATF nor the National Guard will ever get me. They got me once, and they'll never get me again." The ATF no longer had the element of surprise working for them.

They went ahead with their plan anyway, sending helicopters above the compound to distract from the gun-toting agents rushing the building. Koresh answered the door, unarmed (and reportedly smirking), but then closed it when the ATF agents shouted for him to get down. Gunfire broke out from both sides—though it is disputed who fired first. A team of agents climbed ladders to the second floor, broke into a window, and were met with heavy fire. Four agents were killed, and several injured. Six Davidians were killed too, including one who was returning from an errand and attempting to enter the compound from the outside. At one point, a frantic Davidian called 9-1-1, pleading for the shooting to stop, to spare the women and children inside of the compound. A cease-fire was eventually arranged.

Realizing the need to treat the siege as a hostage situation, the FBI took over the next day. They cut off all communications between the compound and the outside world, permitting the Davidians to speak only with their negotiators. But Koresh didn't want to come out. He subjected negotiators to hours of his "Bible babble" that got them nowhere. Over the next few weeks, twenty-one children and fourteen adults were released from the compound (the adults were arrested immediately), but there were still over eighty Branch Davidians inside, and the authorities were growing impatient.

Over Koresh's protests that he wasn't coming out until God gave him the go-ahead, the FBI baited him with tactics such as turning off electricity inside the compound and blasting it with bright lights and loud music at night. This increased pressure just agitated Koresh and his followers, making the situation even more unstable. The FBI feared they could have a Jonestown-like murder/suicide situation on their hands if they weren't careful (see page 139 for more details on that), but Koresh repeatedly denied that would happen.

Koresh finally said that he and his followers would surrender when he was finished writing a manuscript on the secrets of the Seven Seals, but the FBI just saw it as another delaying tactic. On April 19, 1993, they released tear gas into the compound, hoping to flush out the Davidians. Again, their efforts were unsuccessful. The Davidians fired guns in retaliation, though it did no good, as their attackers were ensconced in tanks. Walls of the compound were penetrated by tanks, causing some buildings within to collapse. Fire broke out and quickly spread. It wasn't long until the entire compound was burnt to the ground. Nine residents emerged during the blaze, some suffering serious burns. The rest of the Davidians, including David Koresh, perished. Like Jesus, he died at age 33.

Over twenty years after the tragedy, there is still controversy over how the fire started. Did the Davidians set it to be in control of their own fate? Or did the FBI's tanks knock down lanterns set up due to the lack of electricity in the compound? Autopsies found that Koresh and some others died of close-range gunshots to the head. A group of women and children, huddled together in a building in the center of the compound, died when a tower fell on the building and buried them in the rubble. If the FBI had negotiated in a manner more respectful of the religious beliefs of the Davidians, would they have been able to get them all out alive? What happened in Waco was a massacre that still leaves many mysteries. ▲

# DOOMSDAY DUPES

Here are the stories of a few other doomsday prophets and the folks who were ready to follow them until the end.

## THE SEEKERS

APOCALYPSE: DECEMBER 21, 1954

Dorothy Martin was a Chicago housewife who claimed to have received messages from beings of a planet called "Clarion," warning her that an imminent disaster was due to fall upon humanity. Martin attracted a small group of followers, called the Seekers, who were committed to her prophecy. They left behind jobs and families and gave away money and possessions to prepare for their departure on a flying saucer that was to rescue the group of true believers.

Unbeknownst to the Seekers, social psychologist Leon Festinger and his colleagues infiltrated the group, wanting to see how it would play out if the UFO never came. The seekers gathered at Dorothy's house on the big day, expecting the spacecraft to land in her backyard. They were stunned when it never showed.

Dorothy was distraught, but managed to pick up a message from Clarion that justified their efforts: "The little group, sitting all night long, had spread so much light that God had saved the world from destruction." These events became the basis of Leon Festinger's book *When Prophecy Fails*, a classic work on the phenomenon of cognitive dissonance.

## HEAVEN'S GATE

APOCALYPSE: MARCH 26, 1997

In the early 1970s, Marshall Applewhite foundeded this cult destined for space. Heaven's Gate viewed death as simply a means to reach the "Next Level," when the members would be transported to an alien spacecraft following the Comet Hale–Bopp. At the time the earth was about to be "recycled," or wiped clean and rejuvenated, the Heaven's Gate gang decided it was time to make their exit.

In a rented mansion in an upscale San Diego neighborhood, Applewhite and thirty-eight of his followers gathered for a meal of Phenobarbital (a heavy barbiturate) mixed with applesauce, which they washed down with vodka. They all donned identical black shirts and sweatpants, brand new black-and-white Nikes, and armband patches reading "Heaven's Gate Away Team" for their UFO adventure. And they didn't forget the interplanetary toll: When the authorities found them dead in their bunk beds, each corpse carried a five-dollar bill and three quarters in its pockets.

## UNIFICATION CHURCH
### APOCALYPSE: 2000

Lots of people, from evangelical preacher Jerry Falwell to famous physicist Isaac Newton, predicted that the world would end in 2000. The Reverend Sun Myung Moon, self-proclaimed messiah and leader of the Unification Church, said that 2000 was the year that evil would be banished from the world and the Kingdom of Heaven would be established. However, he'd been wrong about a few things before (he supported US president Richard Nixon during the Watergate scandal, for example).

The Moonies, as his followers were commonly known, were notorious for conducting mass wedding ceremonies all over the world, sometimes marrying tens of thousands of couples at once. If you've ever dreamed of a big wedding, Sun Myung Moon would've been happy to include you among the happy couples and would even match you with a partner if need be—but he died in 2012.

## CRECIENDO EN GRACIA
### (ENGLISH TRANSLATION: GROWING IN GRACE)
### APOCALYPSE: JUNE 30, 2012

José Luis de Jesús Miranda of Miami, Florida, claimed to have become Jesus in 1973. He was an unlikely messiah, a former heroin addict who drank, smoked, and traveled in fancy cars throughout the time of his ministry. De Jesús claimed to be Christ, then turned around and insisted that he was also (somewhat paradoxically) the Antichrist, and his devotees showed their support by getting "666" tattooed on their bodies. He promised them that in 2012, following the collapse of the world's governments and economies, they would undergo a transformation that would enable them to fly and walk through walls. De Jesús never did get to see his apocalyptic vision realized, but his own world ended in 2013, when he died of cirrhosis of the liver.

## MESSIAH FOUNDATION INTERNATIONAL
### APOCALYPSE: 2026

This organization, founded by Pakistani spiritual leader Riaz Ahmed Gohar Shahi, combines Christian, Muslim, Jewish, and Hindu prophecy, with Shahi as the messianic figure. The MFI caused outrage in Pakistan, where MFI members of the group were charged with blasphemy against Islam and a death sentence was issued for Shahi. In 2001, Shahi fled to England to avoid persecution in Pakistan, and some believe him to have died in 2003. But there's still time to be saved—Shahi's followers find his face visible on the moon, and they have faith that he will provide salvation for humanity when the end comes. We'll find out for sure if we live to see 2027 ... ▲

*In order to gain access to this dining room, you have to: (a) say hello to the doorman, (b) slip the maitre d' a cool $10,000 or (c) know Donald Duck's middle name. (Answer: b)*

# CLUB 33

FOUNDED: *1967*

STATUS: *Still open, unlike some other vintage Disneyland attractions, such as the Crane Bathroom of Tomorrow.*

EXCLUSIVITY FACTOR: *At Disneyland, nobody is as big a VIP as Mickey Mouse, but these club members come close.*

SECRECY FACTOR: *Only members are allowed full access, but recently, the park started running a tour called "Walk in Walt's Footsteps," which offers tour-goers a peek at the club's lobby.*

THREAT FACTOR: *Lower than a ride on the Mad Teacups.*

QUIRK FACTOR: *There aren't many places with a $10,000 annual membership fee where you can hang out with costumed characters.*

## HISTORY AND BACKGROUND

Even the happiest place on earth has secrets. As you stroll through Disneyland's New Orleans Square, you might forget you're in Anaheim, California, and not the French Quarter. With all the music-playing pirates walking around, you may not notice the unassuming door (painted a thoroughly unremarkable color referred to by Disney designers as "noseeum") bearing a mirrored plaque with the number 33. This is the entrance to Disney's exclusive Club 33.

Unlike most Disneyland attractions, Club 33 is not for kids. It's an elegant dining club with a price tag that's decidedly not family friendly. It's also the only place at Disneyland where booze is served. So, why does a theme park need a club like this?

When Walt Disney attended the 1964 World's Fair, he visited many corporate VIP lounges and was inspired to create something similar at Disneyland. His secret apartment in the park above the firehouse on Main Street wasn't roomy enough to accommodate many guests (though the ones who were lucky enough to visit sometimes had the privilege of sliding down the fireman's pole to the firehouse below). He needed a place where he could entertain the park's most distinguished visitors in high style. And like so many of his fantasies, Walt made his dream of this private club come true.

Unfortunately, Walt Disney died five months before Club 33 opened in 1967, but the place bears his signature nonetheless. Walt and his wife chose many of the antiques displayed there, along with stills and props from Disney movies. But the man behind the mouse neglected to name the club before he passed away. The official line from the Disney Corporation is that the club is simply named for its address at 33 Royal Street. But there are a few other theories. In 1966 and 1967, the park had exactly thirty-three corporate sponsors, including Coca-Cola, Frito-Lay, and Monsanto, and some folks surmise that that is where the club got its moniker. Another more whimsical interpretation is that the number 3 turned on its side resembles a pair of mouse ears—could the two 3s represent Mickey and Minnie? And yet another explanation is that Walt Disney was a 33rd degree Freemason (a degree unique to the Scottish Rite variety of Masons). Some decorative elements in the club's floors and windows resemble those in Masonic lodges.

We may never know the real reason behind the name of the place, but for those who can get into Club 33, it's an experience that provides all the magic of Disney, and more.

## MEMBERSHIP REQUIREMENTS

It goes without saying that members of this club are Disney fanatics. *Rich* Disney fanatics. Getting into Club 33 requires an initial fee of $25,000, plus annual dues of $10,000. It's a testament to the allure of Disney that so many people are willing to pony up that kind of cash that there's a decade-long waiting list. But in 2012, in honor of the club's 45th anniversary, a limited number of openings were added to the roster of about five hundred members.

For a shot at getting in, one must send a written request to be put on the waiting list—and then be very, very patient. Once accepted, members may bring guests to join them for meals at the club, and they can even arrange for costumed Disney characters to show up! (Less fortunate Disneyland visitors looking for a photo-op would give their mouse ears to have Mickey, Donald, or Goofy appear on command.) Members also enjoy behind-the-scenes access to park attractions, such as private tours of new or refurbished rides. And of course, the possibility of dining next to a famous guest, of which there have been many, is a thrill. Club 33 truly offers the royal treatment on Royal Street.

# INSIDE CLUB 33

The Old World atmosphere of New Orleans Square continues inside Club 33. There is a gorgeous glass elevator in the foyer called the French Lift, which was inspired by an elevator Walt Disney spotted in a New Orleans hotel on one of his trips to purchase furnishings for the club. The hotel refused to sell him the lift, so Walt had a replica specially made. After ascending in the lift to the second floor of the club, members enter The Gallery, where the décor includes a phone booth from the 1967 Disney movie *The Happiest Millionaire*.

The main dining room is a formal affair, decked out in Victorian splendor with glittering chandeliers and antique bronzes. The Trophy Room, with its dark wooden walls, is for more casual dining. It once was home to several mounted animal heads, as well as some animatronic critters. The hunting trophies have since been removed, but an animatronic vulture remains perched in the corner. Walt Disney's intention was for the bird to converse with diners, but the animatronic features were never used. One slightly disturbing detail of the Trophy Room is the microphones built into the lights above the tables—they were installed so that staff could surreptitiously listen to guests' conversations and anticipate their needs, but they are no longer in use.

Throughout the club, vintage photographs, original pieces by Disney artists, and sketches for park attractions adorn the walls. After dinner, the fireworks over the park can be viewed from the balcony—a highlight of the night for many guests.

The traditions of Club 33 are revered among its members—but changes are coming to the beloved institution. The club is currently undergoing a dramatic expansion and renovation. And as of 2012, members were granted access to a new domain: a clandestine cocktail lounge called 1901. The 1930s-inspired lounge is located in the Disney California Adventure section of the park. It is named in honor of the year Walt Disney was born, and is decorated with many historic mementos. These innovations give Club 33 a less exclusive feel, but it will always be a coveted destination for die-hard Disney fanatics. ▲

# OUTLAWS IN FANTASYLAND

Those who know Disneyland by its squeaky clean reputation have probably never run across a gang of pierced, tattooed folks wearing matching denim vests in line for the Jungle Cruise. Such "social clubs" have become prevalent in the Anaheim, California theme park.

In recent years, like-minded folks who love all things Disney started finding each other via social media and meeting up en masse to visit the park. They distinguish themselves from the average park-goers by dressing in a fashion that's more motorcycle gang than Mickey Mouse—but if you look closely at their denim vests, you'll see they don lots of limited edition Disney pins. "Gang" names are emblazoned across their backs: Black Death Crew, Main Street Elite, Walt's Misfits, The Hidden Mickeys, Disney Resort Imbeciles, and the Never-landers are just a few of the park-roving packs. The adults who form the core of this movement also bring their kids on their excursions, making the social clubs an all-ages affair. Indeed, many members view each other as family and see each other outside of Disneyland for holidays and other social occasions.

Not pictured here: fearsome gang leader Mickey Mouse.

But not all park-goers are charmed by the clubs' camaraderie. Social club members likely dabbled in some subculture before devoting themselves to Disney, and as such, many of them sport wild hairstyles and lots of body art, which can be intimidating to outsiders. Plus, there have been reports of gangs behaving badly, committing Disneyland delinquencies such as line-jumping and smoking pot on park grounds. And some social clubbers can be snobbier than Cinderella's stepsisters when it comes to their Disney expertise. Territorial tendencies have even led to turf wars—conduct hardly befitting in the happiest place on earth!

However, tough as they may look, most Disneyland social club members are peaceful folks who just want to enjoy the park with friends. You can follow their exploits by looking up individual clubs (like the ones named on the previous page) on Instagram or Facebook. ▲

*Masons musing in a mine, 1897.*

# THE FREEMASONS

FOUNDED: *The exact date is unclear, since early records have been lost. The origins of Freemasonry can be traced back to local fraternities of stonemasons throughout Great Britain in the late 14th century, but a Grand Lodge was not established until 1717 in London.*

STATUS: *Active the world over.*

EXCLUSIVITY FACTOR: *Members must possess have high morals and be voted into the lodge by current members, but contemporary Masons aren't terribly exclusionary (except when it comes to women).*

SECRECY FACTOR: *At this point, many "secrets" of this society have been revealed, though members continue to stay mum. Masonic Lodges are often open to the public for community events, but there are certain rooms where only Masons are permitted.*

THREAT FACTOR: *Most likely pretty low—many important historical figures have been Masons, but the fraternity no longer has the political pull it once had.*

QUIRK FACTOR: *Masonic "Easter eggs" pop up everywhere, with references in literature, movies, popular TV shows like* The Simpsons *and* 30 Rock, *and even avant-garde works of art like Matthew Barney's* Cremaster Cycle.

## HISTORY AND BACKGROUND

The formidable Freemasons are the largest and possibly the most well known fraternal organization in existence. They have chapters all over the world, perhaps even in your town. They appear frequently throughout European and American history, counting kings, presidents, movie stars, musicians, sportsmen, astronauts, robber barons, and titans of industry among their membership. So how did what began as a network of fraternities for medieval stonemasons become so widespread and influential?

Constructing massive castles and cathedrals was a dangerous job in the Middle Ages, with no workman's comp insurance coverage if a laborer was hurt. So, the stonemasons of Great Britain formed guilds to take care of sick and injured members as well as the widows and orphans of those who were killed on the job. Non-masons saw the advantages of this set-up— essentially, Masons had each other's backs—and by the 1600s, they, too, were invited to join. And so, the Freemasons evolved from a medieval craft guild into a fraternity.

Masons meet in lodges, which today are often spectacular buildings, but centuries ago, a pub or a member's home could serve as a lodge. In 1717, four London lodges came together to form the first "Grand Lodge" under the tutelage of one Grand Master (elected by his fellow Masons), establishing a lasting structure for Masonic groups everywhere. And in 1813, two English Grand Lodges united to form the United Grand Lodge of England, which led to the standardization of Masonic ritual and procedure.

Over the centuries, Freemasonry has broken off into many different divisions and affiliated groups. In the 1800s, there was a schism between English Freemasonry and the brand practiced in Continental Europe, particularly France. But despite these variations, Masonic ritual is centered around the ascension through three "degrees": Entered Apprentice, Fellow Craft, and Master Mason. A member advances through the degrees by strengthening and improving his character, and memorizing the history and mythology behind the fraternity. Freemasonry may best be described as "a system of morality, veiled in allegory, illustrated by signs and symbols."

# MEMBERSHIP REQUIREMENTS

At the top of the list of requirements for wannabe-Freemasons is a strong and true moral compass. In the 1734 book *Constitutions of the Freemasons*— originally published in 1723, then edited and re-published by Master Mason Benjamin Franklin in 1734, and still used by Masons today—it says:

*The Persons admitted Members of a Lodge must be good and true Men, free-born, and of mature and discreet Age, no Bond-men (slaves), no Women, no immoral or scandalous Men, but of good Report.*

According to this decree, women are officially not permitted to become Masons, but that changed in 1882 when a woman was initiated into a French lodge. "Co-Masonry," as the mixed male and female membership came to be known, spread to England twenty years later, but never really took off the way it did on the continent. Even today, women in the few English lodges that permit them are not considered legitimate Masons by most. There are several organizations for female relatives of Freemasons that share many of the same rituals the same rituals as their male counterparts. The most popular of these in the US is the Order of the Eastern Star, founded in 1850.

Freemasonry claims not to be a religious organization, but all members are expected to believe in God or have a religious faith of some kind. However, not all churches are so keen on having Masons in their congregations, as the group's secrecy has caused some to suspect Masons to be guilty of evil deeds such as Satan worship and plotting world domination. By most present-day accounts, these suspicions are unfounded—the Masonic altar and other ceremonial regalia and the mysterious rituals they practice are just fancy trappings of a group focused on personal development, charity, and camaraderie. Discussion of religion and politics is expressly forbidden at lodge meetings, as it could disrupt the atmosphere of brotherly love.

Aspiring Masons must petition a lodge and be subject to a secret ballot where all members present must approve his application. Even one negative vote can bar a prospective member's acceptance. This process might seem harsh, but surprisingly, the vast majority of applicants are approved. Perhaps most people attracted to the fraternity tend to be good guys. Some of these good guys throughout the ages are listed on page 52.

# INSIDE THE FREEMASONS

There are lots of high falutin' Freemasons, but there are also plenty of regular dudes in the fraternity—garbage men, fry cooks, farmers, teachers, et cetera—recalling the organization's original purpose as a brotherhood of working class men laying stones. In the Lodge, all are united on a common level.

No matter who they are, every Mason must rise through the ranks in the same manner. An intensive question-and-answer session is a part of initiation to each of the degrees, and it gets more involved at each stage as the Mason's knowledge grows. This is where the expression "to give someone the third degree" comes from.

The first degree, Entered Apprentice, symbolizes a kind of spiritual birth, starting out on the path of knowledge. The Entered Apprentice studies with another Mason to learn the basic tenants of Freemasonry, and then must recount these from memory (and the many symbols associated with them) when, at the initiation ceremony, he is questioned by the primary officers in the lodge. Following this interrogation, the initiate kneels at the altar, and with his hand on the Bible or the Volume of Sacred Law, takes the obligation (oath) of an Entered Apprentice, which includes a promise to keep secret everything entrusted to him.

The second degree is called Fellow Craft. In this stage, a man's task is to acquire knowledge and apply it to the building of his character and the improvement of society. Once he achieves this, he can petition to be a Third Degree Master. By the time a Mason is raised to this "Sublime Degree," he has not only demonstrated virtues of fidelity, faith, and fortitude, but also has reached a spiritual level where he is assured that his soul will live on after death.

Perhaps the most arcane Masonic ceremony takes place at the third degree—a drama staged in the lodge based on the legend of Hiram Abiff. This distinguished man was the architect of King Solomon's temple in Jerusalem, a building that is the inspiration for many of the decorations found in Masonic Lodges. Hiram Abiff was allegedly murdered by three disgruntled workers who demanded he reveal to them the secrets of a Master

Mason. Abiff refused to snitch and consequently died a noble death there in the temple. The ritual marking a Mason's entry into the third degree involves a dramatic reenactment of this event.

A Master Mason is also privy to the handshake and password that Masons use to identify one another. The secret's out that the grip is given by pressing the thumb between the joints of the second and third fingers where they join the hand, and the password is "Tubal-cain," the name of another Biblical figure (this one a metal worker). But anyone trying to impersonate a Mason probably won't be able to keep up the ruse for long, as the group has so many symbols, rituals, and secrets that an imposter is unlikely to know. In addition to other fine personal qualities, being a Mason requires a sharp memory!

But lodge life isn't all about solemn rituals. Most men seem to be attracted to Freemasonry simply for the camaraderie it builds between members, and meetings are social events after the business is out of the way. Some Masons close their meetings with a drink and a traditional toast that includes the words:

*Then to our final toast tonight,*
*our glasses freely drain,*
*Happy to meet, sorry to part,*
*happy to meet again.* ▲

# BIG NAME MASONS

GEORGE WASHINGTON, First President of the United States

BUZZ ALDRIN, astronaut

SILVIO BERLUSCONI, Prime Minister of Italy (though he has been expelled due to his wild and unethical antics)

SIMÓN BOLÍVAR, leader of South American independence

MARC CHAGALL, Russian artist

WILLIAM CLARK AND MERIWETHER LEWIS, explorers

DAVY CROCKETT, American folk hero

CECIL B. DEMILLE, movie director

DUKE ELLINGTON, jazz musician

HENRY FORD, founder of the Ford Motor Company

CLARK GABLE, Academy Award-winning actor

FEDERICO GARCÍA LORCA, Spanish poet and playwright

HARRY HOUDINI, escape artist

CHARLES INGALLS, father of Laura Ingalls Wilder

JESSE JACKSON, US Civil Rights leader and politician

RUDYARD KIPLING, author of *The Jungle Book* (as well as many writings inspired by Freemasonry)

HARPO MARX, comedian

WOLFGANG AMADEUS MOZART, composer

SHAQUILLE O'NEAL, NBA basketball star

ARNOLD PALMER, professional golfer

PRINCE PHILIP, Duke of Edinburgh, husband of Queen Elizabeth II

RICHARD PRYOR, actor and comedian

PAUL REVERE, American Revolutionary hero

JOSEPH SMITH, founder of the Latter Day Saint movement

DAVE THOMAS, founder of Wendy's

OSCAR WILDE, Irish playwright, novelist, and poet

THE RINGLING BROTHERS, American circus promoters

# MASONIC SYMBOLS

The Masons are big on symbolism. These cryptic emblems may add to their enigmatic allure, but they likely came into use for practical reasons. At the time of the group's conception in the Middle Ages, most of the population was illiterate, so pictures were necessary to convey data. These are just a few Masonic symbols that can be seen throughout lodges. Many are derived from Judeo-Christian theology or tools actually used by stonemasons.

## LAMB

Traditionally, the lamb symbolizes innocence and purity. Masons are given a white lambskin apron upon initiation. An apron was required for actual stonemasons to keep their clothing clean, but today it is a symbolic reminder for Masons to keep themselves from moral defilement. Deceased Masons are even buried with their aprons.

## THE ALL-SEEING EYE OR THE EYE OF PROVIDENCE

This represents the eye of God, whom Masons call "The Great Architect of the Universe." Apparently he can even keep watch from your wallet, since the symbol is incorporated into the Great Seal of the United States, which is shown atop a pyramid on the US dollar bill. Some believe this use of the symbol is proof of a Masonic conspiracy with roots in the founding of the country.

## MASONIC GAVEL

Much like an auctioneer or a judge, the Master of a lodge uses a gavel to keep order to the proceedings. The Masonic gavel has a rectangular head, is flat on one end, and comes to a point on the other end. Stonemasons used this type of gavel to break the rough edges of stones to fit them into place. Now, it is a Master's emblem of authority.

## MOSAIC PAVEMENT

The ground floor of a Masonic Lodge is decorated with a checkerboard mosaic of black and white stone. Legend has it that Moses used this pattern of stones in the Temple of Solomon, but historians call into question this belief. The black and white stones are interpreted as symbols of the evil and good of human life. The checkerboard mosaic is surrounded by a border of stones of various colors, cut or notched into inequalities resembling teeth, a motif that represents being surrounded by blessings and comforts. This border is known as the Indented Tessel, and is known as one of the "Ornaments of the Lodge," along with the mosaic pavement and blazing star.

## THE BLAZING STAR

The Blazing Star is a highly important Masonic symbol that can be seen in the center of a Lodge's checkered floor. Its significance, however, is disputed. Some say the star represents truth—for, by advancing in knowledge, a Mason becomes like a blazing star, shining with brilliancy in the midst of darkness. Others interpret it as a symbol of prudence, its central placement in the Lodge a reminder to Masons to uphold this virtue.

## SQUARE AND COMPASS

This is the universal logo of Freemasonry, displayed outside of lodges and on Masonic jewelry such as rings and cufflinks. Both of the instruments incorporated in the logo were tools used by stonemasons to create true and perfect lines and angles. Since there can be nothing "truer" than a perfect right angle, the square represents a Mason's moral obligation to be truthful and honest to his fellow man. The compass, then, is symbolic of boundaries. Masons are expected to use wisdom of conduct to circumscribe desires and passions within due bounds. There is usually a letter "G" between the square and compass, which stands for Geometry under the Great Architect of the Universe (God).

## YOUNG MASONS — BUILDING A FUTURE

Freemasonry is sometimes thought of as an old boys' club, but young people, like twenty-year-old Robert Griffith, are welcome to join to keep the tradition alive. Robert is a third degree Master Mason who joined the fraternity as soon as he was old enough to do so, which is eighteen in his home state of California. Here, Robert answers some of our most burning questions about being a Mason.

**What inspired you to join the Freemasons?**

A variety of reasons, really. I was born with a bone disease called Blount's Disease, which caused severe bowing of the growth plates in my legs. I was treated at the Shriner's Hospital for Children [the Ancient Arabic Order of the Nobles of the Mystic Shrine, commonly known as Shriners, is an appendant body to Freemasonry]. Without the Shriners, whom are all Masons, I would never have been able to walk, and would have been in a wheelchair the rest of my life. They performed all of my operations up until I was sixteen without charging my family a dime. I joined to both assist them in their non-profit charities, and make friends with the people who saved my life. Aside from that, every Mason I had met before joining—my grandfather, great grandfather, uncles, two of my teachers, and a close friend of mine—were amazing people who I aspired to be like.

It seems like this would be a lot to absorb for a new Masonic recruit.

**What traits should an ideal Mason possess?**

This is a very good question! There are a lot of traits that would be ideal, because the entire fraternity's goal is to "build" upon yourself and become a better person. Loyalty, kindness, charity, respect, and discipline would all be adequate responses.

**What was your Masonic initiation like?**

Well, I can't really say "Hey, here's what we did," because that wouldn't follow tradition that has been carried out for ages! However, I will say, it was nothing like I'd expected. It involved so much history about the fraternity in general—and so little like the conspiracy stuff everyone buys into. To sum up the entire initiation without giving away what happened: You're asked if you truly want to join, you say yes, they teach you about the fraternity, and you're in. It's a bit more complex than that, but that's the pattern!

**What are meetings like?**

The meetings are very simple. Once a month there is a stated meeting—our lodge is every 1st Thursday. Essentially, you go in, sit down, and talk about business. "What kind of business?!" conspiracy nuts ask me. Well, charity opportunities, lodge bills, and any information about the lodge or brothers (illness, surgery, et cetera). Not much to it but a simple get-together. The nights that are the most awesome is when there is a new brother, or when you can attend someone's raising to a degree, because you can watch the history being taught.

**What's the most valuable thing you learned/gained by being a part of the Masons?**

Agh! This is a hard one! If I *had* to choose, I think I would say that the most valuable things that I've learned are ways to better myself. The most valuable thing that I have gained is friendship. As a Mason, you will never have to worry about being alone. If you're in a really tight spot, you have friends to talk to, and even if you're traveling around the world, you'll have friends everywhere you go!

**Do Masons have any special advantages outside of the lodge that we non-Masons may not be aware of?**

Boy, I wish! As nice as it would be to instantly get a job for being a Mason, or get some sort of secret to the universe—no such luck! However, we do have an obligation to uphold: If someone is in a dire situation (i.e. their life is in danger), we are to do anything and everything in our power to help them. There's a reason we call each other "Brothers." You're instant family!

**What do you do when you meet another Mason out in the world? Is there a special handshake, or other gesture of recognition?**

There is a special handshake, one for each of the three degrees. Each handshake has a name that only Masons will know—a password, essentially. And there are other means of recognition, the most common being the Dues Card—it has your name, your signature, the signature of the lodge secretary, and info of where you attend lodge and if you have paid your yearly membership dues. This is the best way to prove that you are a Mason.

**What was your proudest moment as a Mason?**

My proudest moment was when I became a Master Mason. I've learned so much history and have so much more that I need to study, and to go back and reflect on. But hearing the words that I was now a Master Mason of Hartley Lodge #199 . . . I don't know how to describe it! It is a LOT of memory work, and reaching that level shows your dedication to your friends.

**Tell us something surprising about the Masons that non-members might not know.**

That we are actually planning world domination—one pancake breakfast at a time. Or . . . that we don't control everything, only the important stuff!

All jokes aside, the biggest thing that most non-Masons don't know is the promise that we swear regarding the protection of each other as brothers. You watch out for one another, and would help your brothers and their families and trust them to do the same if the need ever arose.

**Would you recommend the Masons to other young people looking to join a fraternal order? What is the best way to get started?**

Absolutely! But only if they are interested. As a Mason, you are told to never solicit someone to join—it must be of their own free will. Those who are interested can start the process relatively easily. You can look up the lodge closest to you, and by emailing the lodge secretary, giving them a phone call, stopping by at one of their dinners, or talking to a Mason who you know, they can provide you with an application. You fill that out and send it in, and the waiting process begins. The only challenging part is memorizing all of the history once you're in!

Freemasonry is definitely a great fraternity to be a part of. They are great men and have given me emotional support and friendship in a time when I really needed it. ▲

*To find out more about becoming a Mason, check out www.thewindingstairs.com. There, Freemason Juan Sepúlveda hosts a Podcast called geared to young Masons. Also featured on his site is a helpful guide where visitors can find the Grand Lodge of every US state.*

Can you *spot the ghost?*

# THE GHOST CLUB

FOUNDED: *1862*

STATUS: *Active*

EXCLUSIVITY FACTOR: *Formerly, hyper-exclusive; currently, hyper-inclusive*

SECRECY FACTOR: *In the beginning, the club was invisible to all outsiders, but now it's easily detectable.*

THREAT FACTOR: *Non-existent (literally)*

QUIRK FACTOR: *Ghost-hunting is not quite as funny as* Ghostbusters *would have you believe—these guys take it pretty seriously.*

## HISTORY AND BACKGROUND

Today's reality-TV viewers probably associate ghost hunting with people shrieking and bumping into walls while being followed by a shaky camera. But paranormal investigation was once a much more dignified pursuit practiced by Victorian gentlemen who did not have the benefit of night vision goggles (or even monocles). A small group of these men formed The Ghost Club: "the world's oldest organization associated with psychical research."

In the mid-1800s, Spiritualism—a movement fueled by the belief that the living could communicate with the dead—captured the imagination of British and American society. Séances became popular and were even held in the White House by First Lady Mary Todd Lincoln. Mediums convinced the masses that spirits could speak through them, and many became famous.

Spiritualism was of interest mainly to the upper classes, such as the group of fellows at Cambridge's esteemed Trinity College, who began meeting in 1855 to discuss ghosts and psychic phenomena. This group evolved to become the Ghost Club, formally founded in London in 1862.

The Ghost Club investigated hauntings and other Spiritualist phenomena. The select group of men involved (no women were allowed) met over supper to discuss topics such as Egyptian magic, "second sight," and their own supernatural experiences. They kept scant records of their meetings, so members were able to speak freely about their beliefs without fear of ridicule — sort of a "Spiritualists Anonymous."

The members of the Ghost Club, though, were anything but anonymous. Due to the club's origins on the hallowed grounds at Cambridge, many of the greatest minds of the time took part over the years: scientists, academics, politicians, clergymen, and literary luminaries such as Charles Dickens, W. B. Yeats, and Arthur Conan Doyle. This was not a club for your average schlub.

After Dickens died in 1870, the Ghost Club seems to have dissolved, but it was revived in 1882 in conjunction with a new group, the Society for Psychical Research (SPR). The SPR took a more skeptical, scientific approach to verifying or debunking supernatural phenomena, and was more inclusive than the Ghost Club, even permitting women to join. This new direction spooked the members of the Ghost Club, and the avowed Spiritualists remained a more secretive, select brotherhood (they actually called each other "Brother Ghost"), only admitting eighty-two members over the course of fifty-five years.

The Ghost Club survived into the next century, undergoing many organizational changes, which included finally admitting Sister Ghosts. They investigated some of the world's most notorious sites known for paranormal activity, including Borley Rectory (known as "Britain's most haunted house") and Glamis Castle (the dramatically creepy inspiration for the setting of Shakespeare's *Macbeth*). The Ghost Club still exists today and investigates hauntings as well as UFOs, cryptology, dowsing, and other supernatural phenomena.

# MEMBERSHIP REQUIREMENTS

In its early days, the Ghost Club recruited new members by invitation only, but that policy was abolished in 1993. Anyone over the age of 18 with an interest in the paranormal may join today's Ghost Club, and their monthly meetings in London are even open to guests. Once a member, you're in for life . . . and thereafter. Deceased members remain on the Ghost Club roster, and perhaps they even show up at meetings sometimes. Whatever your ontological standing, if you're able to get to a computer, check out their official website at www.ghostclub.org.uk.

# INSIDE THE GHOST CLUB

So what's it like to be a ghost hunter? The club hosts overnight investigations into paranormal activity at various locales. Maybe you've fooled around with a Ouija board, but that's kid stuff to the members of the Ghost Club, who aim to conduct serious research. Many of the volunteers who go on these "vigils" are mediums, and they use sophisticated equipment like a thermal imager and a "Ghost Box" to record electronic voice phenomena (EVP).

The events of one recent investigation give us an idea of the ghost-hunting process. The club was summoned to the Glasgow Royal Concert Hall in Scotland, where there were a number of strange occurrences. Reports included shadows moving around the building, and people sensing someone standing beside or behind them when nobody was clearly visible. Was the place really haunted? It was up to the Ghost Club to find out.

Upon entering each room of the concert hall, the Ghost Clubbers recorded the temperature and listened for strange noises. They were highly attuned to the variations in energy as they moved through the building. In the dark café, one member spotted an orb of light and sensed a "religious connection." It was later confirmed that a church had once stood on that very spot. Another member noted feeling nervous and weak in the knees, and then picked up on the name "Martin." He pictured him to be a white haired man, an important person who had a link to the building—and sure enough, they later found out the architect, now deceased, was named Sir J. L. Martin. But the evidence doesn't always add up so neatly. In the bar, the group sensed a humming sound, which was revealed to be only the ice machine.

Ghost hunting has its thrills, but it can also be tedious and unpleasant. Long stretches of time may pass with no paranormal activity to report. Investigators may experience nasty smells, feelings of nausea, and, in the case of the Glasgow Royal Concert Hall, "negative feelings" around the toilet area.

This particular investigation also yielded reports of growls and grunting, strange white mists, human-shaped shadows, a conversation with a spirit conducted with dowsing rods, and one spirit who was the life of the party when he offered everyone a drink. Over the course of this overnight vigil, the Ghost Club collected enough evidence, in their view, to confirm that the Glasgow Royal Concert Hall is indeed haunted. So if you ever have a chance to take in a concert there, remember what's lurking behind the scenes! ▲

# THE CURIOUS CASE OF
# THE COTTINGLEY FAIRIES

Legendary literary detective Sherlock Holmes is known for solving cases using his extraordinary powers of deduction. But as a member of the Ghost Club, Holmes's creator, Sir Arthur Conan Doyle, was less concerned with logical explanations. Eager to see evidence of the supernatural, Conan Doyle was completely taken in by photographs of purportedly real fairies revealed to the public in 1920.

The mysterious legend of the Fairies of Cottingley endured for generations, until, in 1983, the elderly Elsie confessed that the photos were a hoax—the girls had drawn the fairies (who sported elaborate Parisian hairstyles, which probably should have tipped off the "experts" who reviewed the photos), cut them out, fastened them to the foliage with hatpins, and snapped away.

It's true that this wasn't the age of Photoshop, but why would Conan Doyle—the brains behind the world's greatest detective—sustain such an unshakeable belief in these fairy photos? Like many adherents to Spiritualism, Conan Doyle had suffered many tragic deaths in his family, including those of his wife and son, and may have been longing for a connection to them in the spirit world.

The Case of the Cottingley Fairies is one that the fictional Sherlock Holmes probably would have made short work of cracking, but in real life, people's need to believe often trumps reason. ▲

*The big one seems almost real.*

The gates of Hellfire.

# THE HELLFIRE CLUB

FOUNDED:  *The first incarnation of the club was established in 1719.*

STATUS:  *Disbanded by the early 1800s, though other unrelated groups that go by the same name exist in England and Ireland to this day, and a fictional Hellfire Club incorporating some actual club lore exists in the Marvel Comics Universe.*

EXCLUSIVITY FACTOR:  *High—membership consisted mainly of high society rakes who had money to burn and plenty of time to do it.*

SECRECY FACTOR:  *Medium—the club took pleasure in publicizing the fact that they were a secret society, but never revealed the nature of their secrets.*

THREAT FACTOR:  *Perhaps the biggest threat they posed was to the prostitutes they cavorted with, or to their own bank accounts, since gambling was one of their favorite pastimes.*

QUIRK FACTOR:  *In the 18th century, pretty high. These hell raisers rejected the social mores of their time in favor of raucous drunken behavior, orgies, parodying Christianity, and possibly even devil worship.*

## HISTORY AND BACKGROUND

Suppose it's the mid-1700s and you're a listless, horny guy sitting on a pile of inheritance money and longing for some fun that takes place outside of the drawing room. There were plenty of gentlemen's clubs to join at the time, each focusing on particular interests such as politics, literature, or sports. But what if your interests were a bit more . . . perverse? Then the Hellfire Club might be just the place for you.

The first Hellfire Club was founded in 1719 by Philip, first Duke of Wharton, a prominent English politician and notorious rake. The purpose of the club was to ridicule religion and conventional morality, achieved by the duke and his aristocratic friends by performing mock religious ceremonies and having dinners where they dressed as characters from the Bible and consumed dishes such as "Devil's Loin" and "Holy Ghost Pie." Wharton's club disbanded in 1721, when King George I condemned their immorality. Wharton was removed from Parliament as a result and ended up joining the more respectable Freemasons.

But the Hellfire Club was not extinguished entirely. Sir Francis Dashwood, who had founded many other gentlemen's clubs, revived the Hellfire Club in the 1730s, though it was then known by the Order of the Knights of St. Francis, or eventually the Monks of Medmenham Abbey. These monikers were purely satirical, for Sir Francis and his fellow members were anything but saintly. In addition to mocking Christianity and drinking a lot of booze, they allegedly indulged in more illicit activities, such as orgies and Satanic masses. Unfortunately, details of these scandalous sessions remain a mystery, for the official records of the club were, quite appropriately, burned.

## MEMBERSHIP REQUIREMENTS

The Hellfire Club was an aristocratic institution—its mischievous members included British nobles, such as the Earl of Sandwich, inventor of the eponymous foodstuff, and prominent politicians, including US founding father Benjamin Franklin. The club also admitted women, which was unusual for the era. Since respectable ladies were not supposed to hang out in taverns where the club often met, meetings were also held at members' homes, where their lewd antics could commence unchecked.

There were about forty members of Dashwood's club, with an inner circle of thirteen, most of them long-time buddies of their lascivious leader. They were allowed to bring friends to meetings—preferably loose women, but select men could also sit in, if they were sufficiently depraved and possessed a title and/or a reputation to ruin.

# INSIDE THE HELLFIRE CLUB

Most folks don't appreciate others gossiping about them, but Sir Francis Dashwood and his fellow hell raisers seemed to get a kick out of outsiders buzzing about their secret society. Since official records of the club were destroyed, most of what is known about them is based on hearsay and conjecture.

It is a fact that Sir Francis enjoyed dressing in costume—he even commissioned portraits of himself styled as a Franciscan monk and the pope to lampoon Catholicism. Special outfits were also required at club meetings: white jackets, trousers, and caps for the "brothers" of the society, and the same ensemble in red for the "Abbot," who led their mock religious ceremonies. It's unclear what the ladies wore—apparently, in some cases, not a whole lot.

None other than the Devil himself was purported to be the president of the Duke of Wharton's Hellfire Club, and members referred to each other as "devils," too—but there is no evidence that they actually practiced Satanism. Not so with Dashwood's more controversial crew. They were rumored to celebrate black mass and participate in drunken orgies. They even pioneered the "body shot" by sipping wine out of the navel of a naked young woman at their gatherings.

Not surprisingly, Dashwood's "prudish" wife was not a fan of her husband and his pals partying at their country home at West Wycombe, so Dashwood leased nearby Medmenham Abbey to accommodate their antics. It was there that the group became known as the Monks of Medmenham Abbey. As deliciously decadent as it must have been to carry out occult rituals in this formerly sacred environment, the Monks were destined for an even more unique headquarters—one that was much closer to hell.

Sir Francis was obsessed with Paganism, and the caves under a church in West Wycombe were reportedly once the sites of pagan rituals. So, Dashwood had the network of caves excavated and expanded, a six-year project that was finished in 1752. From then on, the secret society performed their rites by candlelight in their subterranean lair.

You can visit the Hellfire Caves and Sir Francis Dashwood's extravagant estate and gardens. For more information, visit www.hellfirecaves.co.uk and www.westwycombeestate.co.uk. ▲

# SINNERS!

These Hellfire Club members pulled some stunts that very well might have led them to eternal damnation.

## BENJAMIN FRANKLIN: ADULTERER

He claimed to live by thirteen virtues, including chastity and temperance, but it seems that Benjamin Franklin strayed from that righteous path as part of the Hellfire Club, which he joined thanks to his close friendship with Sir Francis Dashwood.

In addition to his more wholesome achievements, including the discovery of electricity and the publication of *Poor Richard's Almanac*, this all-American statesman scored quite a few notches in his bedpost. Having a wife at home didn't curb his womanizing ways. His conquests included a mother and her daughter, and possibly his maid, who may have been the mother of his illegitimate son.

So expert was Franklin in the care and keeping of mistresses that he once penned a piece called "Advice to a Young Man on the Choice of a Mistress." In it, he advises the reader to satisfy his raging libido by getting married—and barring that, sleeping with more experienced older women, "because it is impossible to tell a young woman from an old woman in the dark." Perhaps he learned this in the darkness of the Hellfire Caves.

*Who, me?*

## WILLIAM HOGARTH: HYPOCRITE

Famous for his paintings and engravings that vividly portrayed the ills of 18th-century English society, William Hogarth was one of the few non-aristocratic Hellfire Club members. He was born to a poor, middle-class London family, and even spent a few years in debtors' lodging as a young boy. This background inspired the gritty realism and biting satire of his work, evident in engravings like *Gin Lane*, a condemnation of the evils accompanying the drinking of spirits. It's ironic that Hogarth would produce this and other "modern morality" paintings when he was one of a group of people who weren't exactly upright citizens.

In 1757, Sir Francis Dashwood commissioned Hogarth to paint his portrait, dressed as a Roman Catholic clergyman. In *Sir Francis Dashwood at His Devotions*, the Hellfire leader is depicted in a friar's robe with a halo over his head, leering at a naked, prostrate woman. Two of Hogarth's most popular works, *A Whore's Progress* and *A Rake's Progress*, reflected just the kind of "progress" that was probably going on down in the Hellfire Caves.

## PAUL WHITEHEAD: FIXER

A minor poet, Paul Whitehead's contributions as secretary and steward of the Monks of Medmenham Abbey were major. His love for wine and women drew him to the club's inner circle—and possibly men, as well. There is speculation that he and Sir Francis Dashwood were lovers.

Whitehead's various duties included the procurement of prostitutes; political advisor; speech writing; keeping the wine inventory; master of the minutes; and even blackmail, when it was required to keep the activities of the club's powerful members from becoming public knowledge. Whitehead made sure those secrets went with him to the grave. Three days before his death in 1774, he lit a bonfire in his garden and burned all the books and papers relating to the Monks, a conflagration that went on for seventy-six hours. Once he finished that last duty, he took to his bed and died, likely having committed suicide using opium or arsenic.

But Whitehead didn't leave the Hellfire Caves for good. He had his body donated to science and bequeathed his heart to Sir Francis, who kept it in an urn in his mausoleum until it was stolen. Legend has it that the ghost of Paul Whitehead now stalks the caves and will do so until his heart is returned.

## JOHN MONTAGU, 4TH EARL OF SANDWICH: GAMBLER

This sleaze might have been the rakiest of the rakes. He held the lofty position of First Lord of the Admiralty, but was far more interested in gambling, flagellation, and young girls. One of these young lovers was 17-year old Martha Ray, who moved in with the earl and bore him five children after his wife was declared insane in 1767.

But the earl was nothing if not excessive in his endeavors: he also had other mistresses, and other children, and a very dirty mouth. Poet Charles Churchill wrote of the earl:

> *Hear him talk, and you would swear*
> *Obscenity herself was there*
> *And that Profaneness had made a choice*
> *By way of trump, to use his voice . . .*
> *Blasphemy, making way and room*
> *Had marked him in his mother's womb*

His profanity could surely be heard at the card table, for the earl was a profligate gambler. According to legend, his reluctance to take a break from one of his games to eat is what led to his invention of a more convenient meal: the sandwich. But it was his other appetites that earned him the nickname "The Insatiable Earl." ▲

*Aleister Crowley in the hot look for fall 1910: svelte in pelts.*

# THE HERMETIC ORDER OF THE GOLDEN DAWN

FOUNDED: *1888*

STATUS: *Lodges and private practitioners still exist today in limited numbers (no relation to Greece's Golden Dawn political party).*

EXCLUSIVITY FACTOR: *Joining may not be that tough, but to ascend in the order, one must display a mastery of magical theories and practices.*

SECRECY FACTOR: *Over the last century, many of the group's secrets have been revealed, but the Golden Dawn's elusive Third Order is still a mystery.*

THREAT FACTOR: *Hopefully none, if the initiate works their way through the order in the prescribed way—it can be dangerous to practice magic too early, or incorrectly.*

QUIRK FACTOR: *Astrology, tarot cards, and other neo-pagan magical practices have roots in the Golden Dawn.*

## HISTORY AND BACKGROUND

There's an old saying that it's always darkest before the dawn. Members of the Hermetic Order of the Golden Dawn sought to come out of the darkness to find spiritual enlightenment—through magic.

Men of science founded this most influential occult group: three British physicians, who were also Freemasons (see page 47) and Rosicrucians (see page 151). Those organizations had many mystical associations that were folded into the ideas behind the Golden Dawn, resulting in a unique combination of Jewish Kabbalah, ancient Egyptian and Greek myths, several strands of Christianity, and many other esoteric traditions.

The word "Hermetic" comes from Hermes Trismegistus, author of sacred texts on mystical and alchemical teachings arising in the first three centuries A.D. Other groups practiced Hermetic tradition, but supposedly, the Golden Dawn was founded on the basis of a charter from an ancient German Rosicrucian Lodge, which had written a coded record of their clandestine occult rituals. This mysterious document is known as the Cipher Manuscript, and its provenance is suspect—it may have been a forgery by one of the founders of the Golden Dawn, or if it is genuine, the lodge from which it originated was so secret that nobody has been able to prove its existence.

Nevertheless, the "perfectible humanism" philosophy behind the Golden Dawn—the idea that everyone could control his or her destiny with lots of hard work and a little bit of magical power—was compelling enough to attract many well-respected thinkers of the time, including Irish poet W. B. Yeats, English writer E. Nesbit, occultist Aleister Crowley (see page 82), and author Bram Stoker.

In its Victorian heyday, the Golden Dawn held meetings at the Isis-Urania Temple in London, the Amen-Ra Temple in Edinburgh, and the Ahathoor Temple in Paris. Some smaller temples existed, but many of the estimated three hundred to five hundred members met in private homes.

The magical order began breaking down when the leaders of various factions bragged that they alone had contact with the "secret chiefs" of the elusive Third Order—the highest level of the Golden Dawn. These beings, said to be imbued with superhuman powers, were never seen by the group's regular members, and their contacts reported conflicting information from them.

In 1900, a "great schism" occurred when the London temple broke ties with the Paris temple. Different factions of the group began publicly outing each other, and the Golden Dawn was no longer a secret. Scandal further increased their visibility in 1901, when a couple in Paris was accused of recruiting teenage girls to the group for purposes of "sex magic."

What's more, in 1914, Aleister Crowley, bitter about not being admitted to the Second Order, revealed the secrets of the Golden Dawn's initiation rituals in his serial publication *The Equinox*. By this time, the Golden Dawn had splintered into many other groups, including the Alpha et Omega, the Stella Matutina, and the Independent and Rectified Rite. More schisms occurred in the 1920s and 1930s, until finally dying out in the 1970s. There are still some Golden Dawn lodges and independent practitioners today, but there is no longer any central authority for the group.

## MEMBERSHIP REQUIREMENTS

The Golden Dawn welcomed both men and women, which was rare for the Victorian age. Wannabe-Golden Dawn members, or Aspirants, must work through a series of "grades" which are divided into three orders, each indicating a position on the Tree of Life. The four grades of the First Order are related to earth, air, water, and fire, respectively. Aspirants must literally aim for a certain "grade" by passing a written exam on the metaphysical meaning of each of these elements.

Then, if a Lodge's Circle of Adepts consents, the Aspirant is admitted to the Second Order. This is where the fun starts. At this stage, the Aspirant is taught the basics of practical magic and may be made an Adept with the power to initiate Aspirants into the First Order. And as members master magical techniques and move up in grades, they may choose a special area of magical expertise—sort of like choosing a college major.

In the Second Order, Aspirants are pretty high up there on the tree of life. But if they want to ascend to the Third Order, they may not be able to stay on that tree—because entering the Third Order essentially requires dying. Many Golden Dawn adherents believe that no living person can "cross the abyss" that separates mundane life from union with the Divine. However, others believe simply extinguishing the Ego—symbolized by a demon known as Choronzon—grants one entry to the elusive Third Order. Aspirants to the grades of this order have acquired great magical powers. And to reach the final level is to achieve virtual Godhood. Not many manage to make *that* grade.

# INSIDE THE GOLDEN DAWN

All in-fighting aside, the goal of the Golden Dawn was spiritual development, a higher state of being. This process begins with a "banishing ritual" that has become a preliminary for most Western magic. The Lesser Banishing Ritual of the Pentagram entails bringing a dagger to the center of a pentagram, making many gesticulations with the body, "vibrating" several "names of power," including archangels, and visualizing the embodiments of the names recited. This, and other magical rituals, can be performed at an altar outfitted with Egyptian-inspired ephemera and magical tools such as the aforementioned dagger. An altar may be in a Golden Dawn temple, or many practitioners today have altars in their homes.

Golden Dawn members practice many different kinds of magic, including circle casting, astral projection (out of body experience), astrology, theurgy (religious magic), and more. The classic Rider-Waite tarot deck was actually invented in 1909 by Golden Dawn member A. E. White and illustrated by fellow member Pamela Colman Smith. Alchemy—an ancient tradition that includes the ability to transform base metals into gold or silver—is also allegedly practiced by some high-level Golden Dawn magicians. This practice in particular relates to a Hermetic principle—the alchemical process requires a closed, or "Hermetically sealed," container. Though greed is against the Golden Dawn philosophy, one can't help but wonder if some aspirants want in just to get the golden touch!

Many secrets of the Golden Dawn have been revealed over the course of the last century, but there are many others known only by members. For those seeking to become "more than human," the Hermetic Order of the Golden Dawn may be the right place to start. ▲

# THE CRIMES OF MR. CROWLEY

Regarded as the father of modern occultism, Aleister Crowley's falling out with the Hermetic Order of the Golden Dawn was but one incident in a lifetime of scandal and nonconformity. He was born to a wealthy British family in 1875, and broke out of the confines of stuffy Victorian society to become a ceremonial magician, poet, painter, novelist, and mountaineer. Crowley founded his own religion called Thelema, which employed the motto "Do What Thou Wilt." In Crowley's case, the things he was "wilt" to do were often considered depraved and debaucherous. Here are a few of his most notable transgressions.

## HOMOSEXUAL ACTIVITIES

At the turn of the 20th century, homosexuality was still illegal in many places, but Crowley delighted in breaking all the rules. While enrolled at Trinity College, Cambridge, he took a holiday to Stockholm, where he had a transformative mystical experience said to be brought on by his first homoerotic encounter. Then in 1897, he began a relationship with Herbert Charles Pollitt, president of the Cambridge University Footlights Dramatic Club. Herb apparently couldn't tolerate Aleister's interest in esotericism, and the two broke up, much to Crowley's regret. Crowley's homosexual, or, more accurately, bisexual proclivities also didn't go over well with the members of the Hermetic Order of the Golden Dawn, and contributed to him being ousted by the society in 1899.

## PORNOGRAPHY

Crowley's first book was a collection of sexually explicit poems called *White Stains*, published in Amsterdam in 1898. It was called "the filthiest book of verse ever written," and most of the original 100-copy print run was destroyed by British customs. But *White Stains* was not only a celebration of sexual taboos—it also warned readers of the less pleasurable side of things. One poem vividly describes the pain of catching the clap, exclaiming

"How sore it is!" Crowley would go on to have many of his subsequent writings banned and burned, and his work is still frequently contested today.

## MARRYING HIS FRIEND'S SISTER

Nobody wants their sister to marry a guy nicknamed "the Beast." Even though painter Gerald Kelly was a friend of Aleister Crowley, he took issue with being his brother-in-law. The two men met during college at Cambridge, and in the early 1900s were part of the same crowd in Paris, mixing with the likes of writer W. Somerset Maugham and sculptor Auguste Rodin. Kelly introduced Crowley to his sister, Rose, who confided to the occultist that she was having an affair with a married man—but to her sorrow, that would soon have to end since her family had betrothed her to an American. In a gentlemanly yet libertine move, Crowley offered to take Rose's hand in marriage and allow her to conduct her affairs with whomever she pleased. The couple eloped the next morning, much to her family's shock and dismay. However, Aleister and Rose surprised themselves by falling in love. Crowley came to rely on his wife's magical intuition—he was convinced that the Egyptian god Horus spoke to him through Rose. Sadly, their love affair did not have a happy ending. The couple divorced in 1909, and in 1911, Aleister had Rose committed to an asylum for alcoholic dementia, a condition she struggled with until the end of her life. Meanwhile, her brother led a much more socially acceptable existence than his old pal Aleister by becoming a favorite painter of the British royal family, and being knighted in 1945.

## IMPERSONATING ROYALTY

Crowley had a flair for the dramatic. He often assumed false identities of a royal or ancient mystical nature, using titles he claimed were bestowed by European or Hindu aristocracy. After marrying Rose Edith Kelly in 1903, the couple took an extended honeymoon with a stop in Cairo, Egypt. There, Crowley donned Persian garb and passed himself off as a prince named Choi Khan (Hebrew for "the Beast"). His new bride was his princess. They rented an apartment in which Crowley set up a temple room and began invoking ancient Egyptian deities and studying Arabic and Islamic mysticism. Incidentally, "Princess" Rose was pregnant on this trip, and in 1904 she gave birth to a daughter, whom they (anti)christened Nuit Ma Ahathoor Hecate Sappho Jezebel Lilith (a name that is basically a crime in itself).

## ADULTERY

It comes as little surprise that a man obsessed with "sex magick" (he put a "k" at the end of "magic" for reasons relating to numerology) had no qualms about cheating on both his first and second wives. He also welcomed the affections of married women, such as Mary Alice Rogers, whom he met on a ship to Hawaii. He celebrated their brief romance in a series of poems, published as *Alice: An Adultery*, in 1903.

## BLOOD SACRIFICE

In 1909, Crowley went to the Sahara Desert to perform an invocation of Choronzon, the Demon of Dispersion—a being whom Crowley believed to be guardian of "the Abyss," the gap between the Real and the Unreal. To provide the life essence, the spirit needed to materialize, a black-robed Crowley slit the throats of three pigeons and drained their blood at each point of a triangle drawn in the sand. Choronzon allegedly did make an appearance within the magic triangle, channeled through the body of Crowley. Such activities caused many to speculate that Crowley was a Satanist who practiced human sacrifice. That was one crime Crowley was not guilty of—murder and violence were against the law of Thelema—but he enjoyed the sensationalist rumors, and even jokingly referred to masturbation as child sacrifice. According to his diaries, Crowley performed this "sacrifice" one hundred and fifty times a year.

## FAKING HIS OWN DEATH

That killer sense of humor was again in evidence when Crowley pulled this stunt: In 1930, he traveled to Lisbon, Portugal, and left a suicide note atop the rocky cliffs on a seaside chasm called *Boca do Inferno*. It appeared that

*Crowley, pre-belch, with still life.*

"the wickedest man in the world" (as he was dubbed by the British press) had ended his own life by jumping into the mouth of hell. Crowley hoped the ensuing publicity would drum up sales for his books. His friend, celebrated Portuguese poet Fernando Pessoa, was in on the joke, and fed the media frenzy by saying he had seen Crowley's ghost the next day. But other friends of Crowley's were shocked when they heard news of his death. Several weeks later, he revealed his suicide to be a cruel joke when he showed up unannounced at an exhibit of his paintings and drawings in Berlin. Real funny, dude.

# CURSING

No, not the profanity kind of cursing, though Crowley did use some pretty spicy language in his writings. Legend has it that he placed a curse on his physician, Dr. William Brown Thompson, for failing to provide him with sufficient amounts of morphine. Crowley was originally prescribed heroin for asthma, and had struggled with opiate addiction for many years thereafter. Dr. Brown began treating him near the end of his life, continuing him on his regimen of morphine. But Crowley was unsatisfied with the amount the doctor allotted him, so he tried to weasel more morphine out of the pharmacist—behavior perfectly befitting a man who once wrote a book called *Diary of a Drug Fiend*. After that, Dr. Brown always accompanied his persistent patient to the pharmacy. Finally, the doctor stopped prescribing the morphine altogether, which could not have been pleasant for a longtime addict like Crowley. When Crowley died on December 1, 1947, Dr. Brown was found dead in his bathtub within twenty-four hours of his patient's demise. Scotland Yard confirmed that both men died of natural causes, but nonetheless, rumors circulated that Crowley had placed a death curse on the disagreeable doctor—one last wicked act before he left the world.

# NOT GIVING A F**K

The central doctrine of Crowley's philosophy of Thelema was "Do what thou wilt shall be the whole of the law." Thelemites were encouraged to get in touch with their "True Will," and follow their own unique path in life. This concept has influenced freethinkers for over a hundred years. In the countercultural movement of the 1960s, many luminaries paid Crowley tribute. The Beatles featured him among their personal heroes on the cover of the album *Sgt. Pepper's Lonely Hearts Club Band*; Led Zeppelin's Jimmy Page was such a fan of Crowley that he purchased the occultists' house in Scotland; and LSD guru Timothy Leary saw his drug experiments as a way of continuing Crowley's work. Aleister Crowley's legacy as a man who unapologetically did as he pleased will no doubt continue to inspire open-minded oddballs for years to come. ▲

Rumors that the walls also have ears are as yet unconfirmed.

# THE ILLUMINATI

FOUNDED: *1776*

STATUS: *Possibly still active today.*

EXCLUSIVITY FACTOR: *Only the rich, the royal, the famous, and other widely influential folks are part of the Illuminati . . . no plebeians.*

SECRECY FACTOR: *They're very stealthy—believers rely on cryptic symbols and signals from members that the group even exists.*

THREAT FACTOR: *Potentially, pretty damn high. If the Illuminati is real, then it could theoretically take over the world, enslaving the less fortunate members of society, all under the kind tutelage of the Antichrist.*

QUIRK FACTOR: *From your favorite hip-hop stars to the money in your wallet, the Illuminati is everywhere!*

## HISTORY AND BACKGROUND

If you're reading this book, chances are you are open to the idea that there may be shady groups pulling the strings of power—either that, or you want to mock those who fall for such conspiracy theories. The subject of the Illuminati often sparks a debate between those two camps, mainly because it's unclear whether or not the group even exists.

It's clear that a secret society called the Illuminati did once exist, in Enlightenment-era Bavaria. The Age of Enlightenment, beginning in the late 17th century, was a cultural movement that saw European intellectuals coming forward to challenge institutions such as the Church and the Crown. They valued individualism and reason over such fusty traditions, and they promoted scientific method as the basis for advancing knowledge. The Enlightenment was a time of revolution in human thought—and so, when Adam Weishaupt, a Bavarian professor, founded a movement that aimed to eliminate prejudice, superstition, and the Catholic Church's influence over government and cultural affairs, it attracted many followers.

Weishaupt established the Order of the Illuminati (Latin for "Enlightened") in 1776 with just five people, but membership swelled to over two thousand in the next decade, with branches in most European countries. Many members were poached from existing Masonic orders. But some perceived the "enlightened" thinking of the Illuminati as too anti-authoritarian. The group was even rumored to be behind the French and American Revolutions. The Bavarian Illuminati was suppressed by government edict in 1785, and Weishaupt was banished from the country. Membership dwindled until, by the end of the 18th century, the order ceased to exist.

. . . Or did it? Some folks think the Illuminati didn't dissolve, but instead went underground, and are working to establish a New World Order, or a totalitarian world government. If the Illuminists realize their goal, they will control currency, culture, education, government—just about every facet of life. It may sound crazy, but many conspiracy theorists believe it's in the reach of the world's richest and most powerful people.

## MEMBERSHIP REQUIREMENTS

You can't join the Illuminati—you must be born into it (or possibly recruited when you become super successful). Membership supposedly consists of descendants of thirteen of the world's wealthiest families, including the Kennedys, the Rockefellers, and the Rothschild banking dynasty.

Even the Disney and McDonald families are suspected to be in league with the Illuminati. They maintain their power with arranged marriages between families, like European royalty (indeed, some alleged members are actually European royals).

It is true that many world leaders are distantly related—the majority of US presidents, for instance, share a common ancestor—so maybe that part of the conspiracy isn't so hard to swallow. But it gets weirder. There are those who believe that the beings in these bloodlines are not even human, but reptilian humanoids.

These lizard people allegedly come from outer space and can shape-shift into humans—and not just any humans, but the world-dominating elite kind. The internet is teeming with videos of everyone from Hillary Clinton to Justin Bieber revealing their reptilian sides with slitted snake-like eyes or "melting" faces—supposedly evidence of them morphing between forms.

How did these reptilian rumors get started? The notion of shape-shifting has ancient origins. Many cultures believed in gods taking on different forms in the human world. Quetzalcoatl, for instance, was a deity worshipped by the Aztecs. This feathered serpent controlled the boundaries between earth and sky, and had associations with Venus, a planet connected to both agriculture and warfare. And multiple dragons of Chinese legend traveled aboard clouds from the earth to the heavens. These mythological reptilian deities with cosmic connections have a modern-day equivalent in the extraterrestrial lizard people of the Illuminati.

The reptilian rage has been perpetuated by British pop "scholar" David Icke, who commands great sums of money for his books and presentations about this worldwide conspiracy (though Icke was one of the folks who warned that the world would end in 2012, so his theories are more than a little suspect). Even lots of believers in the Illuminati shy away from the idea of lizard people. But if you ever spot, say, the queen of England showing her scales, maybe the myth of the lizard people won't seem so far-fetched after all.

# INSIDE THE ILLUMINATI

So what does the Illuminati actually *do*, besides shifting into reptilian form between cabinet meetings? Well, rule the world, basically. Attendees of the annual Bilderberger Conference of global elite (see page 9) are suspected to be Illuminati. So are many power players in the entertainment industry, who have the ability to convey mind-control techniques via music and movies. The goal is to bring about a New World Order—a world ruled by one authoritarian government made up of the few people from Illuminati bloodlines. Some speculate that the Illuminati has Satanic associations and that the Antichrist will usher in this New World Order.

But you don't have to be a theologian to see evidence of the Illuminati. The establishment of international alliances such as the United Nations and the World Bank; the switch to the Euro from separate currencies for each European nation; and the proliferation of civilian surveillance with technology such as CCTV—in the minds of Illuminati believers, all of these things signal the beginning of the end of sovereign nation states, and a shift to a global takeover by a very small, yet super powerful segment of people.

Think of the Illuminati as a pyramid. The pyramid is actually the preeminent symbol of the Illuminati—you can even see it on the US dollar bill. If the wide base of the pyramid represents the common people of the world, the small tip—adorned with the all-seeing eye, perhaps the eye of Lucifer himself—represents the tiny portion of the population that will rule those below.  ▲

# THE ILLUMINATI'S BRIGHTEST STARS

The Freemasons may have a host of influential members, including many politicians, businessmen, and even founding fathers of the US. But let's face it; those are mostly old white dudes. The Illuminati, on the other hand, has a more glamorous reputation, with a bunch of sexy stars to help pull the strings. Lady Gaga, Lil Wayne, Kanye West, the entire Kardashian family—all have been accused of being Illuminati pawns. Here are some of the other alleged Illuminati adherents you can find spreading their message with their star power.

## JAY-Z AND BEYONCÉ

This power couple is so enmeshed with the Illuminati that they even named their daughter in their honor: Blue Ivy is said to stand for "Born Living Under Evil Illuminati's Very Youngest."

How did such an outrageous story get started? Well, consider the fact that Jay-Z's record label, Roc-A-Fella, is an homage to the name of one of the Illuminati's founding families, the Rockefellers. And the "Roc" hand gesture that Jay and other celebs have been seen flashing might represent the Illuminati pyramid.

And Bey is no innocent bystander either. At the 2013 Grammy Awards, she posed doing the "666" hand sign. Of course, this is pretty much indistinguishable from the hand sign for "OK," so who knows whether Beyoncé was flashing the number of the beast or just feeling good about, you know, being on the red carpet at the Grammys. Illuminati-watchers also cite her aggressive "alter ego," Sasha Fierce, as proof of Beyoncé's demonic possession.

The whole Carter-Knowles clan might be in on the conspiracy. Stories circulated that the 2014 elevator altercation between Jay-Z and Beyoncé's sister, Solange, may have been Illuminati-related. Could it be she found out that her brother-in-law is a cold-hearted snake from another planet sent to conquer the world?

## RIHANNA

Since Jay-Z helped launch her career, it comes as no surprise that Rihanna has inspired rumors that she is part of the Illuminati. The provocative singer does little to dispel such chatter—in her video for the song "S&M," the words "Princess of the Illuminati" flash across the screen behind her.

Some see Rhianna's highly sexualized image as proof of demonic possession, and furthers the Illuminati's Satanic agenda. In the video for her first big hit, "Umbrella," RiRi can be seen posing inside of a pyramid in the shape reminiscent of Baphomet, a goat-like creature whose head is a common Satanic symbol (Beyoncé has also been seen wearing a ring with this little goat guy on it).

Rihanna insists that she is Christian and has denied Illuminati involvement—the reference in the "S&M" video was apparently meant to be tongue-in-cheek—but the rumors persist nonetheless. Even her on-again/off-again relationship with abusive Chris Brown was attributed to the Illuminati, who purportedly paired the two with the intention of an arranged marriage. Is that true? Maybe not, but the idea of it is definitely scary.

## EMINEM

What if an artist refuses to be an Illuminati slave? It was speculated that this was the case with controversial rapper Eminem. He rose to fame under the mentorship of Dr. Dre, who expressed his own Illuminati paranoia in his song "Been There, Done That":

> *Ain't tryin' to stick around for the Illuminati*
> *Got to buy my own island by the year 2 G*

While the year 2000 clearly came and went without an Illuminati takeover, Dre may have warned his protégé about the shadowy group. Illuminati watchers see blatant symbolism in the cover of Eminem's 2002 album, *The Eminem Show*.

It depicts Eminem on a stage with the curtain parted, creating the shape of a pyramid. At the top of this "pyramid" is the "I" in Eminem's name, representing the all-seeing eye. Eminem is shown at the bottom of the pyramid, looking pensive and somewhat defeated. Was he being oppressed by the Illuminati, attempting to resist their mind control tactics?

If he was, his attitude may have changed by the time his movie *Eight Mile* and the accompanying soundtrack were released. In the song "Lose Yourself," the lyrics state:

> *The soul's escaping, through this hole that is gaping*
> *This world is mine for the taking*
> *Make me king, as we move toward a new world order*

The rapper's message got even more confused with his 2010 album *Recovery*. On the album insert, he's pictured covering his eye, again representing the all-seeing eye of the Illuminati. But his facial expression looks a little worried and possibly regretful. And the lyrics to "Not Afraid" are about taking a stand against an entity stronger than himself. But then, when he accepted the Grammy for that album, he was wearing a pyramid necklace. Did the Illuminati orchestrate his success?

At present, the conspiracy consensus seems to be that Eminem is indeed in league with the Illuminati, as his 2014 album *The Marshall Mathers LP II* includes a duet with "Illuminati princess" Rihanna, and the song "Rap God," which features some Illuminati symbolism in the video. So, Slim Shady may be shadier than you think.

## BRITNEY SPEARS

This pop icon may be another celebrity who tried to buck the Illuminati system. She's had difficulty doing so after being raised a bonafide showbiz kid under the influence of the Illuminati from an early age. Conspiracy theorists believe she is a victim of "Monarch programming"—the systematic use of trauma on subjects for mind-control purposes. This process could have begun when Britney joined the cast of *The Mickey Mouse Club* at age 13. Walt Disney himself was a Freemason and suspected Illuminist who secretly worked for the government, and his empire has been associated with the occult and mind control since its beginning in the 1930s. It's possible that the ritual programming that Britney and other child stars were subjected to may have even gone on after hours at Disneyland!

Once programmed, Monarch subjects mindlessly respond to certain triggers or symbolism. In other words, they become Illuminati slaves. Brit even has a song called "I'm a Slave 4 U." But in the mid-2000s, she began behaving erratically—a possible sign that she was trying to break free of her mind-controlling handlers. In 2004, she married twice (and neither husband seemed like the type to get the Illuminati's blessing). In subsequent years, her parenting skills were criticized when she was seen doing risky things such as driving a convertible without a seatbelt and a baby on her lap. Her mental health seemed to hit rock bottom in 2007 when she impulsively shaved her head and attacked a paparazzo's car with an umbrella. But was it a nervous breakdown, or was brainwashed-Britney just thinking for herself for once?

After weathering a stay in a psychiatric hospital, a custody battle for her children, and an extended conservatorship giving her father complete control of her assets, Britney seems to be back on track as far as her career and sanity go. But then again, there are signs like the 2011 video for "Hold It Against Me" that may indicate she is still a victim of Illuminati mind control. In the video, we see Britney seemingly trapped in a room full of TV screens and hooked up to IV lines, reminiscent of being drugged in the Monarch programming process. From this, it looks like this manic Mouseketeer may never escape her Illuminati-controlled media prison. ▲

Two Templars being burned at the stake. Bystanders are like "meh."

# THE KNIGHTS TEMPLAR

FOUNDED: *1120*

STATUS: *Dissolved in 1312, though some suspect the order survives to this day.*

EXCLUSIVITY FACTOR: *To achieve Templar knighthood, one must have been a brave warrior and intensely committed to the Christian faith.*

SECRECY FACTOR: *At the height of their influence, the Knights were world-renowned, but their secret meetings and initiation ceremonies never sat well with the Pope.*

THREAT FACTOR: *High for their targets, medieval Muslims.*

QUIRK FACTOR: *The mysteries of the Order are speculated upon in bestselling books such as* The Da Vinci Code *and films such as* Indiana Jones and the Last Crusade *and* National Treasure.

## HISTORY AND BACKGROUND

The Poor Fellow-Soldiers of Jesus Christ, otherwise known as the Knights Templar, is a pretty humble name for a group that had great power in medieval times and lasting historical impact to this day. The story of the Templars begins in 1095, at the start of the Crusades—a series of wars for the Holy Land that took place over the course of more than two centuries. Jerusalem had been captured by Muslims in 634 and had been under Islamic rule ever since. This posed a problem for Christian pilgrims, who, after their long, arduous journeys to the holy city, were often plundered, pillaged, and even killed upon arrival. Even if they were spared these abuses, they were charged a hefty tax to enter sites like the Holy Sepulchre (the tomb of Jesus Christ). Many were too poor to afford the price of admission and were forced to turn back to their homelands, their pilgrimages all for naught. Finally, in 1099, under the leadership of the Roman Catholic Church, outraged Christians banned together and conquered Jerusalem for themselves.

But there was still danger along the roads to the Holy Land, so around 1120, a group of knights calling themselves The Poor Fellow-Soldiers of Jesus Christ united to protect pilgrims from the dangers they might encounter along the way. Though considered a religious order, the knights were not affiliated with any church, so the king of Jerusalem granted them headquarters in the royal palace on the Temple Mount, where the Temple of Solomon once stood. It is for this reason that they became known as the "Knights Templar."

The Templars' noble deeds earned them a certain celebrity, and soon Christians everywhere were clamoring to join their holy fraternity. No longer were the Templars simply pilgrim escorts, they had taken on the role of defenders of all of Christendom and its sacred sites. It's a bit surprising that so many people wanted to join up—for, when they were not out being noble and valorous, the Knights Templar lived an austere existence with restrictions on every facet of life, including meals, bedtime, communications with friends and family, and even speaking. Incidentally, the fanatical Muslims they wanted to exterminate had similar practices.

The Templars fought in subsequent crusades, a band of fierce warriors fueled by faith. When they won a battle, they were celebrated as heroes. When they lost, they were mourned as martyrs. For a long time, it seemed like the Knights Templar could do no wrong. In 1129, they even earned the endorsement of the Catholic Church, who were at first skeptical that a military order could be considered a religious order. One Pope praised them as "far famed and most valiant champions of the lord."

It was around this time that new recruits, money, and gifts began pouring in from all over Europe. Nobles donated land and estates in exchange for the remission of sins. Templars were given special tax exemptions and legal leniency. And soon, the order that began as "poor fellow soldiers" became rich. Very, very rich. They built mighty fortresses and churches all over the world, many of which are still standing today. They oversaw agricultural estates, or preceptories, throughout France, Italy, Spain, and England to fund their endeavors. They could use their fleet of ships to sail to places such as the Island of Cyprus (the site of their temporary headquarters), which they also owned. To those who idolized the Knights Templar, these acquisitions seemed well deserved. But then the knights made a move that Jesus probably wouldn't approve of: They became usurers, or moneylenders. With their vast wealth, the Knights Templar were the go-to guys for nobles and monarchs to hit up for a loan.

The order's financial power translated to political power, but it was only a matter of time until one of their dealings went sour. King Philip IV of France was already deep in debt with the Templars when he asked them for another loan to finance a war. The Templars denied his request, infuriating Philip. The king was determined to take down the Templars and strip them of their riches.

By this point in the early 14th century, the Knights were no longer the unstoppable military force they once were and did not have the same degree of popular support. Lay-people were sick of the alms collectors sent around by the Templars to collect money for their work in the Holy Land. Just what, exactly, were these supposedly noble knights doing with all of their money? It seemed that their piety had given way to profiteering.

Furious King Philip brought other charges against the order, including heresy, blasphemy, treason, improper religious practices, and sodomy. On October 13, 1307, he had all of the Knights Templar in France arrested (according to legend, this is the reason Friday the 13th is considered unlucky). Most confessed to these charges under torture, but they later recanted. Still, it was too late, and King Philip had many Templars burned at the stake. In 1312, the Pope formally disbanded the order.

# MEMBERSHIP REQUIREMENTS

First and foremost, as it was a religious order, wannabe-Templars were required to take an oath of chastity, obedience, and poverty. Even men who were married had to give up sexual relations with their wives, as their rulebook included a stern warning to "shun feminine kisses."

However, it is possible that masculine kisses were permitted, or even encouraged, in the order. There is speculation that homosexual activities were practiced during the Templar initiation ceremony, and later, upon interrogation, many knights did not deny this.

But that may have been the only fun the monk-like Templars were having. Though it's meant to be a hearty endorsement of the Order, Holy Abbot St. Bernard described them as such in his discourse "In Praise of the New Chivalry":

> *An insolent expression, a useless undertaking, immoderate laughter, the least murmur or whispering, if found out, passeth not without severe rebuke. They detest cards and dice, they shun the sports of the field, and take no delight in the ludicrous catching of birds (hawking), which men are wont to indulge in. Jesters, and soothsayers, and storytellers, scurrilous songs, shows, and games, they contemptuously despise and abominate as vanities and mad follies. They cut their hair, knowing that, according to the apostle, it is not seemly in a man to have long hair. They are never combed, seldom washed, but appear rather with rough neglected hair, foul with dust, and with skins browned by the sun and their coats of mail.*

Clearly, hair care was not a priority. But the big reason to join the Templars was that, in exchange for a lifetime of service, they were guaranteed a ticket to Heaven if killed while battling enemies of the Christian faith.

# INSIDE THE KNIGHTS TEMPLAR

It was a point of great pride to don the iconic Templar uniform: a white mantel emblazoned with a red cross. The Templars were distinguished as one of the most skilled military orders in the Crusades.

However, the business of crusading was not that cut and dry. Templars stationed in the Holy Land became friendly with some local Arabs and understood that at times they needed to cooperate with Muslims. Newbie warriors from the west spoiling for a fight were critical of the order's methods and frowned on their perceived arrogance. Many complained that the know-it-all knights appeared somewhat apathetic when it came to recovering lost ground and defending Christianity from its foes; while others argued that the knights were *too* aggressive, and often wound up fighting with those who would otherwise convert via more peaceful methods.

Though many of the allegations later made against the Templars are dubious, it seems certain that they did let greed get in the way of their original mission. They were accused of spending more time acquiring property and raking in profits than giving charitable gifts, as a religious order was expected to do. And there is a myth that they once failed to capture a Muslim fortress because greedy Christian leaders had been bribed by Muslim gold to raise the siege. This gold subsequently turned out to be copper.

Still, the greatest glory for the Knights Templar was to die fighting for their god. What they were not prepared for was dying for their mortal sins. Could it really be true that these defenders of Christendom actually denied their faith in Christ during their initiation ceremony? That they worshipped idols? That they trampled and urinated upon the Crucifix? That they defrauded their patrons? In medieval times, the fastest way to find out was through the use of torture.

King Philip had the knights stripped of their habits and chained in dungeons. They were subjected to brutal torture methods, including being crushed under iron weights or stretched upon the rack until shoulders and hips were dislocated. It is no wonder that under such conditions, hundreds of Templars confessed to appalling crimes in exchange for their lives. The ones who recanted were burned alive at the stake, all the while shouting their innocence and love for Jesus Christ.

Whatever corruption might have existed among the Templars probably did not permeate the whole band of Christian soldiers, but nevertheless, in 1312, Pope Clement dissolved the order. Its property and surviving brothers were passed on to other more reputable religious orders.

The Knights Templar left behind many mysteries. Whether they're guilty of the crimes they were accused of remains unsettled. There is speculation that before their persecution and capture, the knights managed to hide away some treasure. Could it be that they unearthed the Holy Grail while occupying the Temple Mount, or harbored a secret capable of destroying the Catholic Church? Many Templar symbols and traditions are still used by societies such as the Freemasons, which leads some people to believe that the order of the Knights Templar still survives in some manner. One thing is sure: These icons of medieval times will forever remain a subject of fascination. ▲

# OUCH! FIFTY SHADES OF FAITH

The Knights Templar led a stringent, God-focused existence that didn't include much in the way of fun and frivolity. Modern folks desiring to experience a touch of Templar in their own life might want to try out Opus Dei.

The Catholic institution Opus Dei was founded in Spain in 1928 by the priest Josemaría Escrivá. Opus Dei translates to "work of God," and members, do this work by striving for holiness in everyday life through strict adherence to the teachings of the Roman Catholic Church. Catholic doctrine loosened up in the 1960s, with the passage of a series of reforms known as Vatican II. But Opus Dei rebelled against those reforms, preferring the oppressive old-fashioned ways of the church, including hearing mass in Latin (sometimes multiple times a day). Consider it extreme Catholicism.

While most non-clergy Catholics only sacrifice certain pleasures during the pre-Easter season of Lent, Opus Dei members deny themselves comforts every day by taking cold showers every morning and sleeping on a board, on the floor, or without a pillow. Some even practice mortification of the flesh—self-flagellation as a path to sanctity. While self-injury is considered a mental health issue by most of the population, for Opus Dei members, whipping their own buttocks or back with a strap or wearing a spiked chain around their thighs is said to bolster self-discipline and is seen as a way to imitate the life of Jesus.

Warm and fuzzy it's not, but Opus Dei's influence is growing. There are Opus Dei members all around the world, but the group is strongest in Spain and Latin America. Some followers are ordinary people who strive to do the "work of God" in their daily life, both at home and at their jobs. But a certain segment of followers, called numeraries, commit to a life of celibacy, turning over their salaries to Opus Dei and living in one of the group-run centers, where male and female members are segregated. In 2002, the Catholic Church recognized the contribution of Opus Dei by canonizing its founder, now known as Saint Josemaría Escrivá.

To outsiders, Opus Dei is seen as elitist and enigmatic. But for the steadfast, hard-working acolytes of Opus Dei, "no pain, no gain" is religion done right. ▲

The Lily Dale Museum: a primo piece of real estate in the haunted housing market.

# THE LILY DALE ASSEMBLY

FOUNDED: *1879*

STATUS: *Active*

EXCLUSIVITY FACTOR: *Visitors welcome, but only members of the Spiritualist church can live there year-round.*

SECRECY FACTOR: *In a town filled with psychics, there are no secrets.*

THREAT FACTOR: *Low, unless you're hiding some deep, dark thoughts that you don't want anyone to know.*

QUIRK FACTOR: *Medium. Literally.*

## HISTORY AND BACKGROUND

How are you spending your summer vacation? How about checking into the Divine Wisdom Center, attending a spiritualism rap session, taking a stroll down the Fairy Trail, then stopping at the Inspiration Stump? All of this is possible with a visit to the little hamlet of Lily Dale, New York. The Lily Dale Assembly is the World's Largest Center for the Science, Philosophy, and Religion of Spiritualism, and welcomes an influx of visitors every summer. During Lily Dale's annual summer season, thousands of spirit seekers visit the village to consult with mediums and to attend a "series of events and experiences to bring information, enlightenment, hope, and peace to those who open their hearts to receive."

The basis of the Spiritualist religion is the belief that the soul continues to exist after the death of the physical body and can communicate with the living. Spiritualists endeavor to take individual responsibility for life circumstances, to find the truth in all things, and to live their lives in accordance therewith. Some, but not all, Spiritualists are mediums and/or healers.

The Spiritualism movement began in the mid-1800s, when groups of "free thinkers" began exploring lifting the veil between worlds. The movement picked up steam in 1848, when sisters Kate and Margaret Fox claimed to have made contact with a spirit haunting their farmhouse in Hydesville, New York. The spirit communicated with the girls through a series of knocks and tapping noises. People travelled from far and wide to hear the "spirit rapping," and before long, the Fox sisters gained international fame, performing public demonstrations that attracted both amazement from believers and outrage from skeptics. The girls later admitted that their "gift" was a hoax, but then recanted. Nevertheless, the seeds of Spiritualism had been sown. Demonstrations of mediumship, such as séances and automatic writing, became popular (and profitable) pastimes.

In 1879, members of the Spiritualist church in Laona, New York, purchased eighteen acres of land and founded a religious membership corporation called the Cassadaga Lakes Free Association. In 1906, this Spiritualist camp was renamed Lily Dale after the lilies that grew around the nearby lake. What began as a site for a one-day picnic where Spiritualists would gather to discuss their beliefs grew into a permanent community comprised of charming Victorian cottages and public meeting spaces. In 1916, the Fox sisters' farmhouse was moved from Hydesville to Lily Dale, but was burned down in 1955. Today, Lily Dale has about 275 year-round living residents—though, presumably, residents who have moved on to the afterlife have not necessarily left town.

## MEMBERSHIP REQUIREMENTS

Securing a spot in this special little town is just as tough as facing any big city co-op board. To join the Lily Dale Assembly, you must be a member in good standing of a recognized Spiritualist church for one year prior to submitting your application. There is an application fee and yearly dues. Applicants are required to submit four letters of recommendation (people you've impressed with your predictions might make good references) and meet with the Lily Dale Assembly Board of Directors, who make the decision regarding acceptance. After becoming a member of the Assembly, registered mediums can provide readings for a fee. They are also eligible to purchase a home in Lily Dale.

## INSIDE LILY DALE

Even non-Spiritualists can appreciate the beauty of this tranquil hamlet. Visitors to Lily Dale pay a gate fee and may visit for the day, or stay longer at a hotel, guesthouse, or camping site on the grounds. They can schedule a private consultation with one of many mediums or participate in a free group reading, performed daily during the summer season.

They may also participate in a wide range of workshops, including "Orb Phenom—Orbs Are Among Us!"; "Opening the Third Eye"; "The Spirituality of Food"; "Manifesting Your Mate"; "Decoding the Enchanted Landscape"; "The Beginners Guide to Crystal Energy"; "Paranormal 101"; "Seeing Past Lives With Your Spirit Guides"; "Show Me My Aura"; and "Spoon Bending."

All ages—and species—can get in on the afterlife action, with a Children's Week and a Pet Remembrance Celebration held at Lily Dale's Pet Cemetery. For more information about the goings-on in this unique community, visit www.lilydaleassembly.com. ▲

# ASK A MEDIUM

Gretchen Clark is a 5th generation Spiritualist who has been a registered medium at Lily Dale since 1976. Here's her insight into living and practicing there.

**What does your work as a medium entail?**

A lot of spiritual counseling, communicating with those in spirit and helping them communicate with their loved ones here on the earthly plane.

**When did you first realize you had the gift of clairvoyance?**

Clairvoyance is seeing clear things in the future sometimes, or seeing spirit, not mediumship. It is a different sense. According to my mother, I have always seen and talked with spirits.

**What are the top five most frequently asked questions from visitors?**

1. Is my father/mother/husband/wife/child all right?
2. Is there a heaven?
3. Do animals come back?
4. Can you tell me what is going to happen?
5. Can you answer questions about health?

**What unique insight has being a medium given you about people?**

I think it is how many are oblivious to things around them.

**How did you end up at Lily Dale?**

I grew up in Pennsylvania. My mother and father's people had cottages here, where we would come sometimes in the summer. My parents actually met here, and I met my husband here as well. It seemed a logical place to come and raise children.

**What is special about Lily Dale?**

The energy, the feel of the place, the like-minded people, and the number of those in spirit who are always present.

**Is there a lot of competition between mediums at Lily Dale?**

None.

**What is the most misunderstood thing about mediumship/Spiritualism?**

The most misunderstood thing about mediumship is that people think we are fortunetellers.

About the religion of Spiritualism? I'm not sure. Some people think that all Spiritualists are mediums or healers. I tell them that that isn't true, no more than that all Catholics are nuns or priests. We pray, we believe in God, and of course in an afterlife. Spiritualism teaches personal responsibility; we are responsible for our lives, no one else.

**What was your most notable afterlife encounter?**

When I was ten years old, my father died. It was very unexpected, he was at home and it was in the middle of the night. I was my father's girl, and very upset that we didn't get to say good-bye. One night, a couple of weeks later, I woke up to see him sitting on my bed. He told me that he had come to say good-bye, and that he just didn't get a chance earlier. We talked a bit, and I never again had that same lost feeling. ▲

Denny Chimes, y'all.

# THE MACHINE

## HISTORY AND BACKGROUND

Fraternities and sororities have a lot of influence on some college campuses—but in Alabama, that influence extends to local and even national politics, thanks to a secret society called The Machine. The group began in 1905 as a rogue chapter of Theta Nu Epsilon at the University of Alabama, and it acts as the political arm for a select group of fraternities and sororities. The endorsement of The Machine is almost essential to being elected to the university's Student Government Association (SGA), but beyond that, it has been the starting point for the careers of US senators, congressmen, and many prominent doctors, lawyers, and businessmen.

Before the Machine existed, University of Alabama's fraternity members would compete for campus leadership positions in a ruthless manner unbefitting of Southern gentlemen. So, the boys of Theta Nu Epsilon came up with a way to make the process more civilized: They would seek out students with potential while they were sophomores and then appoint them to the various leadership roles in school organizations. The hush-hush manner in which this was done gave the Machine, as the group became known, a reputation as a secret society that has operated as a sort of shadow government on campus ever since.

The group's most blatant display of power is stacking the student government with Machine-approved candidates. The Machine makes it known to the many fraternities and sororities under its sway who should get their vote. With the numbers drawn from the Greek system, independent candidates are at a severe disadvantage. The Machine almost always wins.

Winning candidates sitting on student government may sow the seeds for post-collegiate leadership positions, but they also serve the Machine's purposes by having people on the inside at the university supporting its agenda. Over the years, this agenda has been rather sinister at times—the Machine opposed campus integration, and when a black man named Cleo Thomas got elected as president of the Student Government Association in 1976, crosses were burned in response.

Thomas had actually managed to beat the election odds thanks to the support of the sororities on campus, who, up until that point, were not officially part of the Machine. After that, Theta Nu Epsilon made room for representatives from the sororities, thus preventing any future backing of independent candidates. When Minda Riley, an independent, ran for SGA president in 1993, she was attacked at night by a knife-wielding masked man and was sent a chilling note reminding her: "Machine rules, bitch."

The Machine now steers clear of making statements with violence, but they are still a force to be reckoned with. In 2013, the Machine became involved with local politics in their college town of Tuscaloosa, Alabama. One of their own, Cason Kirby, a former student government association president, was running for Tuscaloosa City Board of Education, so the proud Greeks of the U of A left campus en masse to cast their votes. This raised controversy and allegations of voter fraud when Kirby's opponent uncovered evidence that some of the voters might have been ineligible. But the Machine that has been working for over a hundred years just keeps chugging along.

## MEMBERSHIP REQUIREMENTS

First and foremost, to become a representative in the Machine, one must be a part of Theta Nu Epsilon or one of the other more prestigious fraternities or sororities at the University of Alabama. Those particular Greeks are usually from reputable, white Southern families—it's rare to find northern newcomers or people of color in their "Old Row" mansions. A pair of representatives from each of these fraternities and sororities is secretly tapped to "go downstairs for the house" or "go underground"—code for becoming a rep in the Machine. But if asked, these chosen few will most likely deny that the Machine even exists, and many Greeks are unaware of who even represents them in the secret society.

## INSIDE THE MACHINE

The representatives of the Machine meet weekly in an undisclosed location. Rumor has it they used to meet in a gravel pit or in the woods near an old Confederate train tunnel, but when those possible locations were revealed in a magazine article years back, they chose a better-hidden headquarters.

At their meetings, they discuss their appointee choices for student government, homecoming queen, and other honors societies. When election day rolls around, the Machine provides transportation to the polls. Frat boys and sorority girls pile into their party buses and limos, where a Machine rep might hand them a beer and tell them who to vote for. Theta Nu Epsilon throws a big-budget after-party for the voters. Some of the Greeks reportedly impose fines on their non-voting brothers and sisters.

But what may be more interesting than what goes on inside the Machine is what happens to University of Alabama students *outside* of it. Fewer than one third of the student body is in Machine-controlled organizations, and many of the other students are fed up with the disproportionate power structure. In 1989, when independent candidate Joey Viselli lost his student government association presidential bid to the Greeks by a small margin, there was thought to be corruption. However, the administration refused to hold another election. In the bitter aftermath, business plummeted at Joey's father's local pizza shop. The place had been popular with the Greek chapters, but after the election kerfuffle, the Machine staged a boycott and soon the pizza shop was out of business. The message: Cross the Machine, and you just might get chewed up in the gears. ▲

# HAZED AND ABUSED

At many schools, hazing is rampant, especially among the Greeks. Incoming pledges are required to perform humiliating and dangerous stunts, often under the influence of a lot of alcohol, all in the name of belonging to the group. Though hazing is illegal in forty-four states, it still goes on—and sometimes leads to terrible consequences.

## SIGMA ALPHA EPSILON, CORNELL UNIVERSITY

In 2011, fraternity member George Desdunes was "kidnapped" by pledges as part of an initiation ritual. While blindfolded, with wrists and ankles bound by zip ties and duct tape, Desdunes and a fellow "captive" were asked trivia questions and forced to do a shot of vodka for every wrong answer. They were also fed a noxious combination of Pixy Stix, chocolate powder, strawberry syrup, and hot sauce. When he passed out, Desdunes's frat brothers tried to carry him to bed, but then opted to leave him in the fraternity library, where he was found dead the next morning. Three students were charged with hazing in the first degree and unlawfully dealing with a child (meaning serving alcohol to a person under 21). To the great dismay of Desdunes's family and friends, his assailants were acquitted of these misdemeanors.

## CHI TAU, CHICO STATE UNIVERSITY

It was "Hell Week" of 2005 on the campus of California's Chico State University—and things were about to get very hellish indeed for Chi Tau pledge Matthew Williams. He was brought to the dungeon-like cellar of the frat house, where the walls were scribbled with the phrase "In the basement, no one can hear you scream." Once inside, he was forced to do calisthenics on a floor that was covered in raw sewage, all while being taunted by the already established fraternity members. As this was going on, Carrington was also forced to drink from a five-gallon jug of water as fans churned frigid air throughout the room. In response, Carrington eventually urinated and vomited on himself before suffering a seizure. He was pronounced dead on the scene when the ambulance arrived. The cause of death was water intoxication, which caused the swelling of his brain and lungs. Alcohol can of course be quite dangerous in this kind of a setting, but this episode shows that even sober hazing rituals can produce terrible results.

## SIGMA ALPHA EPSILON, DARTMOUTH COLLEGE

Dartmouth provided the real-life inspiration for the classic college comedy *Animal House*, so it comes as no surprise that fraternities at the Ivy League college partake in some raucous initiation rites. But Sigma Alpha Epsilon went overboard, according to former member Andrew Lohse. In a 2012 op-ed in the college newspaper, he revealed that in order to be a brother, pledges were made to perform a variety of dehumanizing and stomach-turning tasks, such as "swim in a kiddie pool of vomit, urine, fecal matter, semen and rotten food products; eat omelets made of vomit (called "vomlets"); chug cups of vinegar, which in one case caused a pledge to vomit blood; drink beer poured down fellow pledges' ass cracks." Lohse reported these abuses to the administration and encouraged them to overhaul the Greek system. For this, he became a pariah, shunned by his former frat brothers. But his efforts were not all for naught, as Dartmouth has recently formed a task force on hazing.

## ALPHA KAPPA ALPHA, CAL STATE LOS ANGELES

The boys aren't the only ones getting brutalized—some sororities have initiations just as intense. In 2007, students Kristin High and Kenitha Saafir were pledging Alpha Kappa Alpha, a weeks-long process culminating with a trip to the beach, which involved doing hours of calisthenics on the sand and then walking backward towards the ocean. Kenitha was swept out by a wave, and Kristin went after her. Both girls drowned. The sorority swears that it had nothing to do with it, but it is suspected to be a hazing incident. Still, no charges were bought against anyone in the deaths of these two young women. ▲

*If you or someone you know has a problem with hazing, call the Anti-Hazing Hotline at 1-888-NOT-HAZE.*

Open a window and a flock
of doves might fly out.

# THE MAGIC CASTLE

FOUNDED: *1963*

STATUS: *Open for business . . . magical business.*

EXCLUSIVITY FACTOR: *Only members of the Academy of Magical Arts and their guests may enter.*

SECRECY FACTOR: *This Hollywood landmark was declared a Los Angeles Historic-Cultural Monument in 1989, but the secrets behind the magic tricks performed inside may never be revealed.*

THREAT FACTOR: *Undetectable. Who knows what these magicians are capable of?*

QUIRK FACTOR: *High. Have you seen the outfits some of these magicians wear?*

## HISTORY AND BACKGROUND

You approach the door of an ominous, turreted mansion, your invitation clutched in your hand. You have no idea what is waiting for you inside. You encounter men in capes, flocks of birds appearing out of nowhere, and even a person being sawed in half. You aren't in a house of horrors—you're in Hollywood's famous Magic Castle.

The Magic Castle is the private clubhouse for The Academy of Magical Arts, the world's premier organization dedicated to the art of magic. The Academy of Magical Arts (AMA) was started by William W. Larsen Sr.

in 1951. Years earlier, Larsen had embraced the magical life by founding a magazine called *Genii, the Conjurors' Magazine*, and quitting his job as a defense attorney to perform in a traveling magic show. When he began the AMA, all magazine subscribers were granted membership. After William Larsen Sr. passed away, his wife and older son, Bill Jr., kept the magazine running. But the Academy was languishing until Larsen's younger son, Milt, found the ramshackle three-story Victorian mansion in the Hollywood Hills that would become the Magic Castle.

It took more than the wave of a magic wand to transform the run-down building into a regal retreat for magicians and their friends, but the Magic Castle finally opened its doors on January 2, 1963. At first, the clubhouse consisted of just a bar and a small room where close-up magic tricks were performed. Over half a century later, it contains several showrooms and bars, a restaurant, a séance room, and a music room with a very peculiar piano (more on that in a moment). Aspiring magicians can also take classes taught by some of the world's greatest illusionists.

All of the biggest names in the world of magic have come through the castle at some point: Lance Burton, Criss Angel, Harry Black-

*Harry Houdini in 1905, presumably moments before blowing the photorapher's mind.*

stone Jr. and Sr., Penn and Teller, Siegfried and Roy, and David Copperfield. So it was a blow for the magical community when the beloved institution caught fire on Halloween of 2011—right before a costume party called "Inferno at the Castle." Some noticed strange coincidences connected to Harry Houdini, the most famous magician of them all. The fire began at 1:26 pm on October 31, almost the same time as Houdini's death eighty-five years earlier. One hundred twenty-six firefighters showed up to battle the blaze. And the Houdini Room, which houses the escape artist's straitjacket, handcuffs, and his glass Metamorphosis Chest, was the one room left undamaged. Was Houdini making his presence known? That's just one of the many mysteries tucked inside the Magic Castle.

Luckily, the castle was restored shortly after the fire, and is now open in all its glory. The biggest trick is getting in the door.

## MEMBERSHIP REQUIREMENTS

To have unlimited access to the castle, you must become a member of the Academy of Magical Arts. Those who practice magic as a profession or a hobby are required to test their magical knowledge in an interview with the Academy's membership committee, and then they must shock and amaze the committee members with a demonstration of some magic tricks. The AMA also offers associate memberships to those over the age of 21 who may not practice magic but love it nonetheless, and junior memberships are offered to promising young magicians. In addition to enjoying the dining and performance facilities at the castle, members have access to classes, lectures by world famous magical experts, and a library full of resources on the magical arts.

But the less magical among us can still visit the castle as guests of AMA members. If you've got a magician pal, ask them to pull a guest card out of a hat. You will have to call ahead for dinner reservations—the castle can get really packed on weekends—and adhere to a strict formal dress code (no jeans and sneakers), but once you get inside, the experience is simply spectacular.

# INSIDE THE MAGIC CASTLE

After presenting your guest card and entering the book-lined lobby of the castle, it may appear that you've reached a dead end with no visible doors or hallways. But remember that in The Magic Castle, nothing is as it seems. If you approach an owl figurine perched on a bookshelf and say the magic words, "Open sesame," the wall will swing open to allow you inside.

A Castle Knight may greet you in the Grand Salon, and he'll show you around and share stories of the establishment's colorful history. Look out for magical memorabilia, such as the original trick billiards table from W. C. Fields's stage show in *Ziegfeld's Follies*; a rare program from a Royal Command Performance for Queen Victoria, circa 1855; and an aquarium modeled after Houdini's water-torture cell. Milt Larsen, who can often be spotted holding court in the Owl Bar, calls the castle's unique style of decor "Larcenous Eclecticism."

Perhaps the most mind-boggling piece of furniture in the castle is a baby grand piano that appears to be playing itself. The piano is actually played by Irma, the castle's resident ghost—and she takes requests. Legend has it that Irma was one of seven sisters who lived in the building when it was a private home. Irma distracted the family so much with her eternal practicing on the piano that they banished her to the attic, where she remained until her death in 1932. When the piano was discovered and moved to the Music Chamber, the spirit of the persistent pianist returned as well. Ghosts are notoriously flighty, but Irma is a dependable one—she's always poised at the keys, ready to play any song requested. Castle guests are continually amazed by her seemingly endless repertoire.

Next, you'll want to see a magic show in one of the castle's theaters. Performers in the cozy Close-Up Gallery do close-up magic—sleight-of-hand stuff, like card tricks and disappearing coins. In the Parlour of Prestidigitation, the Victorian parlor show is recreated. A parlor magician performs classic effects such as cutting and restoring a rope, vanishing silks, or levitating a rose. And in the castle's largest theater, The Palace of Mystery, illusionists whose acts require large props and pyrotechnics wow the crowd.

When you're not hypnotized by magic tricks, keep an eye out for famous faces. This is Hollywood, after all, and celebrities regularly appear at the Magic Castle to take in dinner and a show. Currently, Neil Patrick Harris, star of *How I Met Your Mother* and *Doogie Howser, M.D.* (and a hobby magician), serves as president of the AMA.

Magic can truly be found in every nook and cranny of this very peculiar private club. To learn more about visiting or becoming a member of the Magic Castle, go to www.magiccastle.com. ▲

# THE MAGIC OF MARCO

A magician never reveals his secrets, but New Jersey-based magician Marco provided the inside scoop on his profession. Marco made the pilgrimage to the Magic Castle twice over the course of his more than thirty-year career. While visiting the castle with a friend, he did some close-up magic tricks for spectators in the bar. Irma dutifully played "Smoke on the Water," at his request (Marco claims "Irma" is not really a ghost, but he won't divulge how the illusion is done). The highlight of the castle for Marco was sitting in the front row of the Close-up Gallery, only two feet away from his magical idol, Pop Haydn (a past vice-president of the AMA), as Pop performed his funny and awe-inspiring act.

Before Marco became a popular magician, he was a full-time musician—a drummer. In 1975, he and the guitarist of his band took a night school magic class on a lark. It was a good investment—the class was just $40 including props, and over the course of ten weeks, Marco learned the basics of everything he needed to know, including tricks he still practices today. For many years, Marco only did magic shows occasionally; he didn't realize there was good money in it until, while performing at a festival organized by a friend, an agent spotted him and offered to get him some lucrative gigs. Marco dropped his drumsticks and became a full-time magician.

Marco's specialty is close-up strolling magic, which means he'll approach small groups at an event with sleight-of-hand tricks, like making small objects disappear or magically transferring a coin from his hand to the hand of one in his audience. He's also performed street magic to larger crowds at places like New York City's South Street Seaport.

Whatever the venue, it's important for a magician to have the right look. It's all about showmanship. "Being a magician is being an actor playing the role of magician," Marco says. Traditionally, magicians had mostly worn tuxedos, until guys like Criss Angel and David Blaine turned the industry on its head by performing in jeans and T-shirts, much to the chagrin of old

*Marco: already in possession of your keys.*

timers. Marco doesn't go quite that casual—he wears custom-made satin vests with six pockets, important for "pocket management" of magical items used in his act. He accessorizes with magical bling: a gold pin with a top hat, cane, and glove on his left breast; a chain with a gold ball that opens into a Masonic cross around his neck; and a double pocket watch chain on his right waist pocket. Instead of a watch, the chains are attached to a small magic wand with crystals on it and to a gold antique cigar cutter knife. Marco says his look ensures that when he walks into a room, "They know I'm not a male stripper."

Marco has many tricks up his sleeve, but a crowd favorite is called "dollar in fruit." In it, an audience member cuts open a lemon, and Marco miraculously makes a dollar bill appear in it. Most spectators are impressed, but sometimes one will challenge him, saying "You don't have special powers." To this, Marco responds, "You're absolutely right—I don't have special powers, but I do have certain knowledge. And knowledge equals power!" ▲

*To learn more about Magic of Marco, visit www.magicofmarco.com.*

*Citizen Know Nothing, when asked to "face right."*

# THE ORDER OF THE STAR-SPANGLED BANNER/ KNOW NOTHINGS

FOUNDED: *1850*

STATUS: *It fizzled out by the end of the decade.*

EXCLUSIVITY FACTOR: *American-born Protestant men were welcome, but immigrants and Catholics were most definitely not.*

SECRECY FACTOR: *Fairly high—members responded to inquiries about the group with "I know nothing."*

THREAT FACTOR: *Medium—they did manage to get some folks who shared their nativist beliefs into public office, but the popularity of the party didn't last long.*

QUIRK FACTOR: *These are the guys who look for the "Made in America" tag on everything—even people.*

## HISTORY AND BACKGROUND

Look at the melting pot that New York City is today, and it may seem inconceivable that it was the birthplace of a political party dedicated to stopping immigration. Before a xenophobic political party called American Party took the national stage, it began with a secret society called the Order of the Star-Spangled Banner (OSSB). The OSSB was started in New York City in 1850 by a 34-year-old commercial agent named Charles B. Allen. The group's three dozen or so members met in one another's homes during the society's first two years. The issue that bonded them together was nativism— a belief that established Americans are of higher status than newer arrivals.

More than three million foreigners landed on American shores between 1846 and 1855. Nativists—or "patriots," as they thought of themselves—feared economic competition from cheaper immigrant labor, resented the growing political power of foreigners, and insisted that the newcomers were destroying the culture of the United States.

They were especially opposed to Catholicism, the predominant faith of the Irish immigrants pouring into New York City in the mid-nineteenth century. Nativists perceived Catholics as being under the control of the Pope in Rome and, as such, a danger to the American values. They also blamed immigrants, Catholics in particular, for spreading violence, drunkenness, and disease.

But many nativists were wary of airing their distaste for foreigners in public for fear that immigrants would boycott their businesses. This was a legitimate economic threat in New York and other cities such as Chicago,

*Know-Nothing Soap—*
*Perfect for scrubbing "sub-par"*
*Americans out of existence.*

Milwaukee, and St. Louis, where immigrants actually outnumbered native-born citizens. So, it was important to the OSSB that their organization remained secret.

Despite their efforts to be discreet, in 1852 the OSSB came to the attention of an older, more established nativist fraternity called the Order of United Americans, which saw the OSSB as a group devoted to political organizing in the interest of nativist policies. With the support of the Order of United Americans, OSSB membership went from under fifty people to over a thousand in just three months.

Still, the Order remained cloaked in secrecy. When questioned about the group, members were to respond, "I know nothing." Because of this, Horace Greely, editor of *The New York Tribune*, dubbed them the "Know Nothings." Greely didn't mean it favorably, but the name stuck. The Order of the Star-Spangled Banner, once an insular local fraternal club, was now a full-fledged national political party called the Know Nothings, or the American party.

## MEMBERSHIP REQUIREMENTS

Membership requirements stipulated that one had to be a native-born, Protestant, American man, of at least 21 years of age, and willing to obey the Order's mandates without question. For aspiring younger nativists, there was also an under-21 group called the Order of the American Star (a.k.a. the "Wide Awakes").

As the Order grew, secret local councils were formed to receive new recruits. These councils were tasked with performing background checks on potential members to ensure they met all the necessary requirements, being mindful not to expose their purpose or even the existence of the Order in the process. Five blackballs from current members could block any OSSB hopeful from joining. A rejected candidate could be barred from reapplying for admission for six months.

The stringency of these guidelines varied by locale. To join a lodge in New York or Massachusetts, for example, a man not only had to be native-born himself, but his parents and grandparents had to be, as well (though exceptions were made for relatives who fought against the British in the American Revolution). By 1855, the Indiana chapters of Know Nothings were not even required to be native-born, as long as they were Protestant. But plenty of folks made the cut—there were over one million Know Nothings throughout the US at that time.

## INSIDE THE OSSB/KNOW NOTHINGS

Other nativist organizations like the Order of United Americans required members to purchase expensive uniforms and pay significant dues. Not so with the OSSB. The group cost nothing to join and was strictly a political organization, with no benevolent responsibilities. The OSSB also didn't have their own dedicated meeting halls, so their gathering places varied. Sometimes they rented the halls of other fraternal organizations; sometimes they met in members' homes, if space allowed; they were even known to meet in cornfields to avoid notice in small towns where it was harder to keep secrets.

Once they had a place to gather, the initiation process could begin. Initiates were invited to step into the anteroom of the council's meeting place (though it's unclear how this was dealt with in a cornfield) and asked if he believed in a Supreme Being. If he said yes, the questioner asked him to swear he'd never reveal anything that transpired at their meetings. Having taken this oath, the initiate was then asked to confirm that he was at least 21 years of age, a Protestant, not married to a Roman Catholic, and that he would never vote for a foreign-born or Catholic political candidate, regardless of party affiliation.

If his answers were satisfactory, the initiate would be permitted to enter the council's inner sanctum, where he would be briefed on the group's handshakes, passwords, signs, phrases of recognition, and hand signals. After these rituals were completed, the man would then be officially a first-degree member of the order. He could later apply for second-degree status, which was voted on by existing second-degree members, who were eligible to hold leadership positions within the order and be nominated for public office. More nativists in office meant fewer aliens and Catholics in positions of authority.

Not only did the Know Nothings wish to limit political office holding to native-born Americans, but they wanted a 21-year residency period before immigrants could even become citizens and vote. They also advocated restrictions on liquor sales (better to keep those foreign drunks from getting sauced). Their platform was popular enough that the Know Nothings replaced the Whigs as the nation's second largest political party. By 1855, they had taken control of the legislatures in parts of New England and were the dominant opposition party to the Democrats in New York, Pennsylvania, Maryland, Virginia, Tennessee, Georgia, Alabama, Mississippi, and Louisiana. The party had five senators and forty-three representatives in Congress. But by 1856 they were in decline, having been unable to achieve any of their original objectives.

While it wasn't exactly a political Cinderella story, the rhetoric of the Know Nothings and other nativists still echoes today in groups like the Tea Party and other anti-immigration advocates. ▲

# ABE KNOWS IT ALL

The Know Nothing party held an anti-slavery stance, which earned it followers in the North. But President Abraham Lincoln didn't see it being on board with the abolitionist cause at all. In 1855, he denounced the Know Nothings in eloquent terms:

> *I am not a Know-Nothing. That is certain. How could I be? How can anyone who abhors the oppression of Negroes be in favor of degrading classes of white people? Our progress in degeneracy appears to me to be pretty rapid. As a nation we began by declaring "all men are created equal." We now practically read it, "all men are created equal, except Negroes." When the Know-Nothings get control, it will read "all men are created equal, except Negroes, and foreigners, and Catholics." When it comes to this I should prefer emigrating to some country where they make no pretense of loving liberty— to Russia, for instance, where despotism can be taken pure and without the base alloy of hypocrisy.*

# HATS OFF TO TAMMANY HALL

The Order of the Star Spangled Banner was not the only New York City secret society that gave rise to a political movement. Before the political machine known as Tammany Hall began its reign over 19th-century New York, it was an unassuming benevolent patriotic society like many others formed after the American Revolution.

Founded in 1789, the Tammany Society was named in honor of a Lenape Indian chief called Tamanend, and as such, the club had a Native American theme. Its meeting place—a downtown tavern—was referred to as the "wigwam," the trustees were "Sachems," and the president the "Grand Sachem." They were even known to dress in Indian garb at their meetings. By establishing a museum in City Hall dedicated to the preservation of Native American relics, the Tammany society showed that the mock Indian ceremonies weren't just fun and games for them.

But when Aaron Burr got involved in 1797, the group went political. Through the Tammany Society, Burr—perhaps most famous for killing his political rival, Alexander Hamilton, in a duel in 1804—chartered the Manhattan Bank, which helped him amass the funds to campaign for Thomas Jefferson. When Jefferson was elected as the third president of the US, Burr became his vice president, and many Tammany Society members were rewarded with appointments to other important offices.

Tammany Hall's influence on New York City politics became stronger with the influx of immigrants in the mid-19th century. Unlike the Know Nothings, Tammany Hall happily courted the immigrant population for votes, and even served as a sort of public welfare agency, providing food, coal, or rent money to those in need. And they even offered entertainment—for an admission price of fifty cents, visitors at Tammany Hall headquarters in Manhattan's Union Square could see theater, concerts, opera, and puppet shows, or indulge the bar, bazaar, ladies' café, and oyster saloon. This era of Tammany Hall under the regime of powerhouse politician William "Boss" Tweed is the backdrop for the Martin Scorsese movie *Gangs of New York*.

In the mid-20th century, Tammany's power began to wane—accusations of corruption and mob ties, and the advent of New Deal programs offering government assistance that Tammany once provided in exchange for votes eventually brought them down. But the society's legendary reign over New York City, and even the national political scene, will never be forgotten. ▲

Welcome to Jonestown
Peoples Temple Agricultural Project

"Welcome," indeed.

# PEOPLES TEMPLE (JONESTOWN)

FOUNDED: *1956*

STATUS: *Ended in 1978 after its members' mass suicide in Guyana.*

EXCLUSIVITY FACTOR: *Until the mid to late 70s, all were welcome; after that, only the hardcore believers in the "Father" Jim Jones remained.*

SECRECY FACTOR: *High. After the group defected to Guyana, their compound and activities within it were off-limits to all outsiders.*

THREAT FACTOR: *Extremely high. Many people broke up their families and ended their lives for the congregation.*

QUIRK FACTOR: *It gave us the phrase, "Don't drink the Kool-Aid."*

## HISTORY AND BACKGROUND

"I represent divine principle, total equality, a society where people own all things in common, where there's no rich or poor, where there are no races. Wherever there are people struggling for justice and righteousness, there I am." Sounds pretty good, right? Those are the words of Reverend Jim Jones. In 1956, he founded his own church, The Peoples Temple, in his home state of Indiana—but he was never content to be a small town preacher. The Peoples Temple espoused a grandiose message of peace, love, and understanding, through the lens of socialism. In the eyes of Reverend Jim Jones, all were equal, and he wanted his church to be a force in creating an egalitarian society. Northern California was ground zero for progressive politics, so in 1965, Jones left the Midwest and set up shop there.

The Peoples Temple was a hit in California, where it had about three thousand registered members by its high point in the mid-1970s. People of all races and ages were attracted by the charismatic preacher's message of justice and equality, and his efforts to promote civil rights and end the Vietnam War. They were also impressed by his "healing powers." At religious meetings, in his flashy suits and signature aviator glasses, Jones would cure cancers, restore mobility to the disabled, and read minds. Later, these feats were revealed to be hoaxes—the "sick" were parishioners in disguise, and the "cancerous tumors" they expelled were nothing but chicken livers. Jones's co-conspirators in these schemes felt that the deception was worth it if it helped further the church's noble cause.

But despite its idealistic veneer, conditions behind the scenes of the Peoples Temple were less than picture-perfect. Jones had sexual relationships with many members, and he oversaw the beatings of others. Disillusioned ex-parishioners spoke to the press about these abuses, and when media scrutiny intensified, Jones panicked. In 1977, he and hundreds of his followers fled for the small South American country of Guyana, where they established a commune called Jonestown.

Anticipating the need for a haven from the US government and the media, Jones had dispatched fifty followers to clear the jungle and construct the buildings of Jonestown when he purchased the property in 1974. Now, with the arrival of Jones and his followers, population of the remote settlement swelled to nearly a thousand people by late 1978, and living conditions there were not good. Jones continued manipulating and abusing his congregants in Guyana. They had no one to turn to for help—communication with the outside world was restricted, and armed guards surrounded the compound, preventing anyone from escaping.

Meanwhile, back in the States, concerned relatives of Peoples Temple members were pleading with authorities to investigate Jonestown. In November 1978, California Representative Leo Ryan flew to Guyana with a TV crew and various reporters. When Ryan's team was finally permitted into the compound, Jones appeared to be a madman. Fifteen residents clandestinely pleaded with Ryan to take them back to the US. Ryan agreed, and they left together for a nearby airstrip, but before their plane could take off, gunmen sent by Jones opened fire on the group. They killed Ryan, an NBC correspondent, a cameraman, a newspaper photographer, and one of the departing family members.

Jones knew that the murder of the congressman and the others would have severe repercussions—and he had a diabolical plan to avoid that. He instructed his followers to drink cyanide-laced grape Flavor Aid (a beverage similar to Kool-Aid) in an act of "revolutionary suicide." Over nine hundred people died that day in the largest mass murder-suicide in history.

## MEMBERSHIP REQUIREMENTS

First and foremost, Reverend Jim Jones demanded absolute loyalty from his followers. They were to call him "Father," and prioritize their relationship with him above all others. Families involved in the Peoples Temple were split apart—husbands and wives were forbidden from having sex, and children were isolated from their parents and encouraged to "inform" on them. Transgressions, such as doubting Jones's divinity (he claimed to be the reincarnation of Jesus Christ, Buddha, Vladimir Lenin, and others), resulted in being beaten and humiliated in front of the congregation. Punishments became even more severe once the Peoples Temple moved to Jonestown.

On a positive note, racism was not tolerated in the church, and such a diverse group was extraordinary in a time when racial tensions ran high. Jones himself had a "rainbow family," with one part-Native American child, three Korean children, a black child, and two white children. To promote his goal of a multi-racial society, Jones arranged marriages between many congregants, favoring bi-racial partnerships and the adoption or birth of bi-racial children. Ultimately, this was just another way that Jones controlled the sexual behavior of his followers.

Though the majority of church members were black, only white women were inducted into the "Inner Staff"—a select group who acted as Jones's spies, couriers, and assistants in the phony faith healings. Jones had sex with many of these women, and then put them down in front of the others, creating rivalry between them and greater loyalty toward him. Jones also accused everyone of being homosexual—everyone but himself, of course. Followers were encouraged to remain celibate unless "Father" sought out their sexual attention.

Becoming a Peoples Temple member could be a pricey proposition. Members (back when they were working in normal society) were required to give twenty-five percent of their salaries to the church. Some donated all of their property and savings, effectively trapping them in the organization with no place to go. Elderly parishioners left their estates to the church. Much of these funds went toward building Jonestown.

## INSIDE JONESTOWN

The Peoples Temple resembled a cult more than a religious organization. This was never clearer than when Reverend Jim Jones convinced over nine hundred people to follow him to Guyana, leaving family, friends, and jobs behind. Once there, Jones's manipulation and abuse, fueled by his addiction to amphetamines and barbiturates, became worse than ever.

He imposed torturous punishments such as shocking wrongdoers with electric cattle prods, or putting them in coffin-like boxes several feet below ground for extended periods of time. All correspondence going in and out of the camp was censored, and phone calls were strictly monitored, with members coached on what to say. Frantic loved ones had no way of knowing how terrible conditions really were in the camp and feared their friends and family members were brainwashed.

Those desiring to leave Jonestown and go back home had many obstacles in the way. Any word of an escape plan could be reported to "Father" by another Temple member trying to win his favor. And anyone who did manage to get past the armed guards that surrounded the compound had to make their way through the jungle, since Jonestown was located many miles from civilization. But miraculously, few people succeeded in escaping Jonestown and were able to provide information on what happened there.

Rather than the utopian paradise that residents hoped for, Jonestown turned out to be more like a concentration camp. Residents spent long hours doing hard labor on very little sleep. Sometimes they would get no sleep at all, when Jones summoned them out of bed to the main pavilion to listen to him rant about conspiracies threatening to destroy their community. Sometimes during "White Nights," as these occasions were known, members were subjected to suicide drills, during which they were expected to drink vats of liquid that Jones claimed was poisoned as a test of loyalty. After being so broken down physically and psychologically, it was easier for Jones to convince his congregate to follow him to oblivion.

But before that final catastrophe, they had to contend with Congressman Ryan's visit to Jonestown. It began pleasantly enough, with a musical reception in the pavilion and a tour of the settlement, but the tone changed when someone handed a reporter a note that said, "Help us get out of Jonestown." This enraged Jones. The note writer was permitted to leave with her family and a few other members. It's possible that more people would have liked to go, but were too afraid of their volatile leader to risk speaking up.

After the murder of the congressman and the others at the airstrip, Jones knew his warped socialist dream was done for. He served his followers vats of grape Flavor Aid laced with cyanide, ordering them to give the toxic cocktail to babies and children first. When the horrific ritual was finished, over nine hundred people lay dead. Jones himself died of a gunshot wound to the head (most likely self-inflicted).

Jonestown is remembered as the site of the largest murder-suicide in history. A tyrannical leader pushed his followers to a place where they had no other way out. Once their messiah, Jim Jones became their killer. ▲

## "LET'S GET GONE"

On their last day at Jonestown, Reverend Jim Jones addressed his followers in an impassioned speech, urging them to commit "revolutionary suicide." Some protested that they were not ready to die, but Jones convinced them they had no choice. On the recording of the speech, parishioners can be heard both applauding and crying. Here are selections from his chilling diatribe.

. . . How very much I've tried my best to give you a good life. But in spite of all of my trying a handful of our people, with their lies, have made our lives impossible. There's no way to detach ourselves from what's happened today.

. . . If we can't live in peace, then let's die in peace.

. . . Be kind to children and be kind to seniors and take the potion like they used to take in ancient Greece and step over quietly because we are not committing suicide; it's a revolutionary act. We can't go back; they won't leave us alone. They're now going back to tell more lies, which means more congressmen. And there's no way, no way we can survive.

. . . But to me death is not—death is not a fearful thing. It's living that's cursed. . . I'm tired of being tormented to hell, that's what I'm tired of. . . . I'm not talking about self-destruction. I'm talking about that we have no other road. . . .

. . . I made my manifestation, and the world was not ready for me. Paul said, "I was a man born out of due season." I've been born out of due season, just like all we are, and the best testimony we can make is to leave this goddamn world.

. . . Some months I've tried to keep this thing from happening. But I now see it's the will—it's the will of Sovereign Being that this happen to us. . . . It's all over. The congressman has been murdered. Well, it's all over, all over. What a legacy, what a legacy.

. . . Please get us some medication. It's simple. It's simple. There's no convulsions with it. It's just simple. Just, please get it. Before it's too late. . . .

Please, can we hasten? . . . For God's sake, let's get on with it.

. . . It is not to be feared. It is a friend. It's a friend . . . sitting there, show your love for one another. Let's get gone. Let's get gone. Let's get gone.

. . . Don't lay down with tears and agony . . . We must die with some dignity. We will have no choice. Now we have some choice.

. . . Children, it will not hurt. . . . I don't care how many screams you hear. I don't care how many anguished cries. Death is a million times preferable to ten more days of this life.

. . . No, no sorrow—that's all over. I'm glad it's over. Hurry, hurry my children.

. . . Where's the vat, the vat, the vat? Where's the vat with the Green C on it? The vat with the Green C in. Bring it so the adults can begin.

. . . Take our life from us. We laid it down. We got tired. We didn't commit suicide, we committed an act of revolutionary suicide protesting the conditions of an inhumane world.

## BREAKING THE SHACKLES OF BRAINWASHING

People who join cults are seeking empowerment and belonging. They often come from abusive or oppressive backgrounds and feel their individual worth has gone unrecognized. They are people who feel a sense of emptiness and alienation in their lives or a fracture in their support system. They are often seeking to make their lives better and have a desire to help others—so when a person like this encounters a charismatic cult leader who promises these things, it's easy to get hooked. But once a person is drawn into the group, the slow destruction of selfhood begins.

Cult leaders make their followers feel worthy and important to their cause, and convince them that the detractors in their lives are the source of their unhappiness. Followers become increasingly dependent on the group and isolated from mainstream society. Often, they will do anything to uphold the group's ideals, no matter how wrong those ideals are, for fear of punishment or rejection. They may feel they have no other place to go.

But some people involved with cults manage to break free of the brainwashing and move on with their lives. Oregon-based therapist Kristi Erlich specializes in helping former cult members recover from their experiences—a process sometimes called "deprogramming." These are some of the methods she uses to help people disengage from cults.

## DECONSTRUCTING THOUGHTS AND FEELINGS

Many former group members struggle to discern their own thoughts, feelings, and values from those programmed by the group. Their responses to the world have become so automatic that they need to slow down and judge every one of their thoughts, feelings, behaviors, and beliefs against their own inherent system of values. This is possibly the most painstaking part of disengaging because people have been so discouraged (punished, even) for differentiating themselves in any way. They have lost touch with their previous identity and values. To help them, asking simple questions until they are able to rediscover themselves is key. For example, "Is it *actually* bad to talk to the postal carrier? What might happen?" The individual can then follow the questions to their logical ends.

## CONNECTING WITH OTHER FORMER
## GROUP MEMBERS / SUPPORT GROUPS

This may not happen for a long while after leaving a cult. The original trauma the individual experienced was in a group, so people are not likely to feel safe or expose themselves in another group. There is also a perception of profound risk that other former members who the individual confides in may not be fully out of the group and/or will relapse and expose the individual. People guard their freedom and individuation from the group fiercely. But connecting with former members also has great potential for healing, as those who share group experiences have the greatest capacity for understanding and acceptance of the individual.

## FINDING PURPOSE IN NEW LIFE

Helping people see how they contribute to the "greater good" without oppressing or limiting others is critical to disengagement. Offering the individual a perspective on their unique value in their families and community and a sense that grandiosity is not necessary to live with purpose, can be helpful. This can have a positive impact on the shame people feel for abandoning their purpose, as well.

## REALITY CHECKING

People disengaging from groups do not have an accurate sense of what is real about their feelings and experiences. In order to survive in their group, they were expected to believe in truly bizarre and irrational things, forcing them into a kind of suspended mental and emotional fantasy. Simply allowing them to tell stories of their experiences and reacting with compassion and curiosity, rather than judgment, will convey subtle and not-so-subtle messages of reality.

## NORMALIZING EXPERIENCES AND EDUCATING

Talking about the things other people experience when leaving groups can be so helpful. There is often a great deal of relief and emotional catharsis hearing about the shame and alienation experienced by other people leaving groups. It allows the individual to believe that they are not alone and that their feelings make them normal.

## ALLOWING FOR AND ENCOURAGING DISAGREEMENT AND DIFFERENTIATION / INDIVIDUALITY

Identifying and inviting former group members to disagree with their therapist (and others) can offer an opportunity for confidence building and self-empowerment. This sends the message that being oneself is no longer dangerous and is, in fact, welcome.

## REINFORCING AND IDENTIFYING
## HOW DIFFERENCES ARE VALUABLE

Uniformity and conformity are critical structures of any cult or high-demand group. Facilitating thought and conversation about how differences and diversity are critical to the survival of humankind, and that they simply make life more interesting, encourages people to accept and allow for their own unique identity development. ▲

*If you or someone you know is involved in a destructive cult and wants to leave it, contact the Cult Hotline & Clinic: (212) 632-4640 or info@cultclinic.org.*

The Temple of the Rose Cross. Mobile homes were pretty fancy in the early 17th century.

# ROSICRUCIANISM

FOUNDED: *Late medieval Germany, probably around 1407*

STATUS: *Survives through several modern societies formed for the study of Rosicrucianism*

EXCLUSIVITY FACTOR: *In the beginning there were only eight members, but Rosicrucian orders today welcome all "Seekers."*

SECRECY FACTOR: *In its early days, it was very hush-hush; today, almost anyone can join a group.*

THREAT FACTOR: *Hard to say—many, many secret societies, fraternal organizations, and other groups, both malevolent and benign, have allied themselves with Rosicrucianism over the years.*

QUIRK FACTOR: *Followers believe Rosicrucian teachings are the key to the truth, but the entire movement may be based on a fictional character.*

## HISTORY AND BACKGROUND

Once upon a time, in medieval Germany, there was a boy named Christian Rosenkreuz. He was the last descendant of the Germelshausen, a noble family that flourished in the 13th century. They lived in a castle in the Thuringian Forest. The family was followers of Catharism, a radical Christian religion that has two gods: one good, one evil. Their religion was considered heretical by the Catholic Church, and so the whole family was put to death—except for the youngest son. Five-year-old Christian was spirited away by a monk and placed in a monastery, where he spent the rest of his childhood.

As a young man, he set out on a pilgrimage to Jerusalem. But when the monk who was accompanying him died mid-journey, Christian stopped off in Damascus. There, he studied medicine and became renowned for his medical skill. He then traveled to Arabia, where he met a group of wise men who had mysteriously been expecting him. From them, Christian learned Arabic, physics, and mathematics. These sages also introduced him to the *Book M*, which contained the secrets of the universe.

Christian continued on to Egypt, where he studied botany and zoology, and then to Morocco, where he learned about magic and the Cabala. He returned to Germany wishing to spread his mystical knowledge, but prominent European figures of the time were not receptive. So he assembled seven disciples, and the group of eight founded Rosicrucianism, also known as the Fraternity of the Rosy Cross. It was determined that the members would live in separate countries to influence people all over the world and would meet annually in Germany. They pledged to keep their fraternity secret for one hundred years.

Christian lived to the ripe old age of 106, and when he died, he was surreptitiously buried in a hidden tomb under the altar of a temple—a heptagonal chamber Christian had built himself. On the door was an inscription that read: *I shall open after 120 years.* Lo and behold, in 1604, 120 years after his death, the tomb was discovered. Amazingly, the body of Christian Rosenkreuz was in a perfect state of preservation.

Sound like a fairy tale? That's because it probably is. Christian Rosenkreuz (whose last name means "Rosy Cross") is now generally regarded to be a fictional character. His story became known throughout Europe in the early 17th century thanks to the circulation of two manifestos, *The Fama Fraternitatis RC* (The Fame of the Brotherhood of RC) and *The Confessio Fraternitatis* (The Confession of the Brotherhood of RC), documents that ostensibly revealed the secret history of the Rosicrucian order. The manifestos promoted a "Universal Reformation of Mankind."

The ideas in the manifestos were met with much enthusiasm. People believed in the legend of Christian Rosenkreuz and his noble order, even though the manifestos directly state:

*We speak unto you by parables, but would willingly bring you to the right, simple, easy and ingenuous exposition, understanding, declaration, and knowledge of all secrets.*

Nevertheless, the ancient esoteric truths of Rosicrucianism, shedding light on the secrets of the universe and the spiritual realm, have influenced many seekers of wisdom throughout the ages.

## MEMBERSHIP REQUIREMENTS

During Rosenkreuz's lifetime, the Rosicrucian order was said to comprise no more than eight members at a time. Each one was a medical doctor and a sworn bachelor. These men took an oath to treat the sick without payment, to keep their fellowship secret, and to find a replacement for himself before he died. Three such generations are said to have passed before the manifestos would be revealed to the public. By the early 1600s, scientific, philosophical, and religious freedom had grown greatly since the time that the order was supposedly founded two hundred years before. Now that the intellectual climate was right for it, all "seekers" were invited to learn from Rosicrucian wisdom.

Although it incorporates many different spiritual traditions, Rosicrucianism is a quasi-Christian order, and in its early days was associated with Protestantism. The anonymous authors of the manifestos gave no clue to their identity, save that they were Protestants. A curious statement in *The Fama* manifesto even suggests that Martin Luther, the seminal figure in the Protestant Reformation, was an agent of the Rosicrucians:

*In this [Memorial] Table stuck a great naile somewhat strong, so that when it was with force drawn out it took with it an indifferent big stone out of the thin wall or plaistering of the hidden door, and so unlooked for uncovered the door, whereat we did with joy and long-*

*ing throw down the rest of the wall and cleared the door, upon which was written in great letters — Post CXX Annos Patebo (which means At the end of 120 years I will disclose myself), with the year of the Lord under it . . . For like as our door was after so many years wonderfully discovered, also there shall be opened a door to Europe (when the wall is removed) which already doth begin to appear, and with great desire is expected of many.*

Supposedly, that "door"—the tomb of Christian Rosenkreuz—was opened on October 31, 1604. Years before that, on October 31, 1517, Martin Luther nailed a copy of the *95 Theses* to the door of the Castle Church in Wittenberg, Germany, an event now seen as sparking the Protestant Reformation. In Europe, October 31 is celebrated as Reformation Day. Another thing that connects Luther to the Rosicrucians is his family coat of arms, which is similar to the order's symbol of a rose on a cross.

Membership requirements for other Rosicrucian-related organizations vary. A vast array of groups has linked themselves to a Rosicrucian tradition over the years: The Hermetic Order of the Golden Dawn (see page 77), and the Scottish Rite body of Freemasonry are but a few. To join a present-day Rosicrucian-like group, consider the Ancient Mystical Order Rosae Crucis (AMORC): there are lodges all over the world, and members simply pay yearly dues in exchange for access to correspondence courses in Rosicrucian subjects. AMORC invites initiates to "discover how extraordinary you really are."

# INSIDE ROSICRUCIANISM

So, exactly what do Rosicrucians study? Meditation, telepathy, reincarnation, and healing treatments were just a few of the "secrets of the universe" supposedly passed down to Christian Rosenkreuz by the sages of the East. Alchemy is also of interest, but if anyone has ever managed to turn boring old metal into gold, it's remained under wraps. It's important to remember that although he's probably just a character created for the sake of allegory, in addition to being a philosopher, Rosenkreuz was also a doctor. He "left behind" a book for his followers, distilling his scientific and medical knowledge.

The concept of a secret organization on the verge of transforming the arts, sciences, religion, and political and intellectual landscape of Europe was exciting to many people at the dawn of the 17th century. The continent reached the height of Rosicrucian fever in 1622, when two mysterious posters appeared on the walls of Paris within a few days of each other. The first said: *We, the Deputies of the Higher College of the Rose-Croix, do make our stay, visibly and invisibly, in this city.*

It was an appealing concept, which later gave rise to the "Invisible College," a group of natural philosophers around Robert Boyle, one of the founders of modern chemistry. The Invisible College evolved to become the Royal Society of London for Improving Natural Knowledge, commonly known as the Royal Society—a learned society for science founded in 1660 that is possibly the oldest such organization still in existence.

Whether or not Christian Rosenkreuz ever existed, it's clear that the Rosicrucian teachings have a significant impact on the development of the arts and sciences to this very day. ▲

# LOOKING FOR THE MAGIC

The doctrine of Rosicrucianism has influenced many magical traditions. Annabel Gat, who writes under her pen name Licorice Root, is a New York City-based Astrologer whose quest to uncover the mysteries of the universe has exposed her to Rosicrucianism and many other esoteric teachings. Today, she uses that knowledge to do astrological forecasts for Lana Del Rey, 50 Cent, Justin Bieber, and other stars for *MTV News* (as well as many regular folks). Here's what Annabel has to say about Roscicrucianism.

### How were you exposed to Rosicrucianism?

I remember reading a Rosicrucian astrology book at East West Bookstore in Manhattan in the mid-2000s, and being a (very) young and inexperienced Astrologer, it was very inspiring for me to find a book on astrology that went beyond basic western new age astrology concepts. Prior to encountering this book, I was aware of many occult orders; however, finding a book that spoke to my main interest inspired me to search out a local NYC magickal organization to join, which ultimately was the Temple of Thelema [an organization based on the philosophy of Thelema, developed by occultist Aleister Crowley—see page 82].

### How can Rosicrucianism benefit the average person?

Any religious study will benefit the average person because the need to create connections between occurrences and to apply meaning to our experience is satisfied, or at least, stimulated, by religious study.

### How do you use Rosicrucian teachings in your life and work?

Rosicrucianism has influenced and colored my understanding of history and how people throughout time have approached the Great Work [this is the process of using spiritual practices to find enlightenment and fulfillment of one's potential].

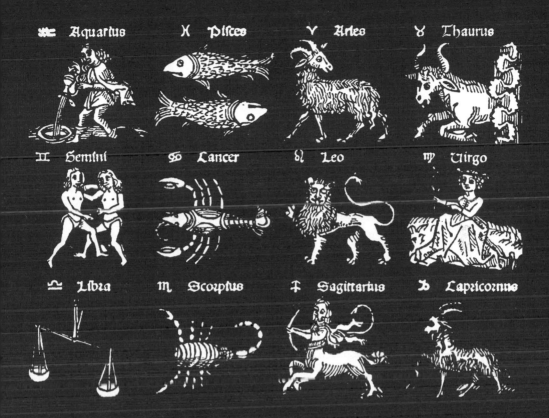

**There are so many facets to Rosicrucianism. What are the most important parts of it to you?**

What I have learned from the Temple of Thelema, Rosicrucianism, and the like is that to keep something secret is to make is sacred. Silence is an important lesson. None of these groups are secret societies because being secret sounds sexy—it's because silence is part of the way we find inner wisdom. ▲

*You can book your own astrology or tarot reading with Annabel by visiting her website, www.rootastro.com.*

"The Tomb" is, if nothing else, an apt name for the club's historical residence.

# SKULL AND BONES SOCIETY

FOUNDED: *1832*

STATUS: *Active*

EXCLUSIVITY FACTOR: *High—only fifteen students are initiated each year.*

SECRECY FACTOR: *Medium—members' names are public, but their meetings and some of their rituals are not.*

THREAT FACTOR: *Potentially high—the members often go on to hold positions in the highest echelons of power.*

QUIRK FACTOR: *Low. Nothing quirky about preppies.*

## HISTORY AND BACKGROUND

Long before Harvard spawned Facebook, there was a much more exclusive Ivy League social network: Yale's legendary Skull and Bones Society. It was founded by two seniors, Alphonso Taft (father of the 27th US president) and valedictorian William Huntington Russell in 1832. Russell was disgruntled about not receiving an invitation to the prestigious academic secret society Phi Beta Kappa, so he retaliated by forming Skull and Bones, which grew to be just as esteemed as Phi Beta Kappa and even more mysterious.

Skull and Bones pays obeisance to Eulogia, the goddess of eloquence—which is ironic, because members are forbidden to speak about the club and are even instructed to get up and leave the room if the society comes up in conversation. Legend has it that Eulogia took her place in the pantheon in 322 B.C., and she returned in a kind of second coming on the occasion of the society's inception. This is why the number 322 appears in the society's skull and crossbones logo.

The society is known informally as "Bones," and members are known as "Bonesmen" (which is better than "Boners"). Just fifteen Bonesmen are chosen from every senior class, but out of this relatively small group has come a disproportionately large percentage of the world's most powerful leaders. Over the years, Bones has included presidents, cabinet officers, spies, Supreme Court justices, and captains of industry.

Indeed, the mystique surrounding Skull and Bones sets it apart from Yale's other secret societies, among them being Scroll and Key, Wolf's Head, Book and Snake, Mace and Chain, and Berzelius. Landed societies, like Bones, have buildings on campus. Their headquarters is a brown sandstone mausoleum known as the Tomb: a crypt-like, windowless structure that is strictly off-limits to non-members.

The most private room in the building is known as the Inner Temple, or Room 322. Behind the locked iron door is a case holding a skeleton that the Bonesmen call Madame Pompadour. Along with her remains, the case contains the society's cherished manuscripts, including the secrecy oath and instructions for conducting an initiation—a ritual in which they are said to use human remains.

There certainly is no shortage of bones inside of the Tomb. It is decorated with dozens of dangling skeletons and skulls and other macabre relics. Chiseled on the walls are German and Latin phrases such as *Whether poor or rich, all are equal in death.*

But while rich and poor may be equal in death, that's not necessarily so in life. The wealth, privilege, and power enjoyed by Bonesmen has sparked many conspiracy theories about the group. Skull and Bones has been implicated in everything from the creation of the nuclear bomb to the Kennedy assassination.

## MEMBERSHIP REQUIREMENTS

Picture this: It's springtime of your junior year, and you're taking a nighttime stroll around campus. Suddenly, you are approached by a group of masked seniors who force you into a black limousine and offer to take you back to their tomb. Would you accept the invitation? Many Yalies would, happily. This process of "tapping" is how Skull and Bones singles out potential members.

"Tap Night" works a bit like the Sorting Hat at Hogwarts in the Harry Potter books—it's when juniors are invited to join the society that is the best fit for them, with Skull and Bones being the most prestigious of the bunch (though disturbingly similar to Slytherin in some ways). Years ago, the tapper would order the tappee to "Go to your room," and then extend the formal invitation to join the club in the privacy of the tappee's dorm room. If the tappee accepted the invitation—and he almost always did—he was promptly inducted into the society that very day.

Tap Night is a slightly more raucous affair these days, with contenders for Skull and Bones and Yale's other secret societies running around campus in Halloween-like costumes. It may be preceded by interviews and "pre-taps," giving the tappers and the tappees a chance to test the waters before committing to a society.

So who gets tapped for Skull and Bones? Historically, young men from the richest and most powerful families were prize picks. Relatives of Bonesmen also got preference. Even in the late 1960s, when many of Yale's other senior societies had adopted more progressive practices, Bones was still a boys' club with a reputation of choosing the same kinds of people, year after year. In an article in the 1968 Yale yearbook, Lanny Davis, a 1967 Yale graduate and a secret society member who would go on to become a White House special counsel in the Clinton Administration, described their selection process as follows:

*If the society had a good year, this is what the "ideal" group will consist of: a football captain; a Chairman of the Yale Daily News; a conspicuous radical; a Whiffenpoof; a swimming captain; a notorious drunk with a 94 average; a film-maker; a political columnist; a religious group leader; a Chairman of the Lit; a foreigner; a ladies' man with two motorcycles; an ex-service man; a negro, if there are enough to go around; a guy nobody else in the group had heard of, ever.*

Today, the Skull and Bones roster is not quite so predictable, nor is it as dependent on class and blood ties. It is still elite and selective, but with a focus on inducting student leaders from various backgrounds. In 1991, they voted to allow women in (by a narrow margin), and recent groups of inductees are usually divided equally between men and women and almost always include Hispanic, Asian, African American, and LGBT students. What these members have in common is that they seem poised to go on to positions of great power, which is the purpose behind this secret society.

## INSIDE SKULL AND BONES

Bonesmen meet in the Tomb two evenings per week, as they have done since the dawn of the order. They spend one of the nights socializing and the other debating cultural and political affairs. But details of what goes on behind Tomb doors are unknown to most outsiders. Because members take an oath of secrecy, persuading one to speak to the press is tough. Alexandra Robbins, author of the Skull and Bones exposé *Secrets of the Tomb*, says that the majority of the Bonesmen she contacted refused to speak to her, and some even harassed and threatened her. However, she did manage to glean this information about their initiation ritual, which apparently features an interesting group of characters:

*There is a devil, a Don Quixote and a Pope who has one foot sheathed in a white monogrammed slipper resting on a stone skull. The initiates are led into the room one at a time. And once an initiate is inside, the Bonesmen shriek at him. Finally, the Bonesman is shoved to his knees in front of Don Quixote as the shrieking crowd falls silent. And Don Quixote lifts his sword and taps the Bonesman on his left shoulder and says, "By order of our order, I dub thee knight of Eulogia."*

Journalist Ron Rosenbaum wasn't permitted such access, so he hid out on the roof of a neighboring building and surreptitiously videotaped a nocturnal initiation ceremony in the Tomb's courtyard. He described it thus: "A woman holds a knife and pretends to slash the throat of another person lying down before them, and there's screaming and yelling at the neophytes."

Rosenbaum has been obsessed with Bones ever since his days at Yale as a classmate to George W. Bush. He longed to get inside their clubhouse. "I had passed it all the time," says Rosenbaum. "During the initiation rites, you could hear strange cries and whispers coming from the Skull and Bones tomb."

Whatever is going on in there, it was once considered very unladylike. "There were rituals that some women would find offensive," says a Bonesman from the 1960s, who refused to elaborate. "Some [alumni] wanted to fight to make sure those traditions didn't have to change." Could he be referring to the longstanding rumor that Bonesmen masturbate inside of coffins? Or something even more sinister?

Though members of Skull and Bones refuse to speak openly about their society to outsiders, they are required to reveal their innermost secrets to fellow initiates. In a ritual called "connubial bliss," the brand new Bonesmen would gather round the fireplace and recount their entire sexual and romantic histories. Today, this ritual has evolved from an X-rated affair to a PG-13 party where each new member delivers an oral autobiography, a time-consuming event meant to forge friendship. Either way, knowing all of each other's deepest, darkest secrets is a kind of protection.

Bonesmen know each other by code names. Long Devil is assigned to the tallest member; Boaz (short for Beelzebub) is bestowed upon anyone who is a varsity football captain. Other names are drawn from literature (Hamlet, Uncle Remus), from religion, and from myth. The name Magog is traditionally assigned to the incoming Bonesman with the most sexual experience, and Gog goes to the new member with the least. William Howard Taft and Robert Taft were Magogs. So was George H. W. Bush, difficult as that may be to imagine—apparently, his undergrad antics would have had Barbara clutching her pearls. Their son George W. was not assigned a name, but invited to choose one. Nothing came to mind, so he was given the name "Temporary," which he never bothered to replace.

George W.'s grandfather, Prescott Bush, made a more permanent contribution to Skull and Bones lore. Bones and other Yale societies have a reputation for stealing from each other or from campus buildings. They have a charming name for this thievery: "crooking." During the first World War, prankster Prescott Bush and some of his fellow Bonesmen are believed to have "crooked" the grave of the great Apache warrior Geronimo. His skull is reportedly kept in a glass case by the front door of the Tomb.

More human remains decorate the interior walls: skeletons, skulls, and other ghoulish ornaments, along with portraits of distinguished members. To continue with the Harry Potter comparisons, it sounds rather like Hogwarts meets haunted house, though a recent infiltrator said the inside of the Tomb looked "something like a German beer hall."

Members of other societies who have managed to break into the Tomb describe a tunnel leading to a chamber with a coffin. There is also a room with candles, a chopping-block, and a basin with two carved skeletal figures leaning over it full of red liquid. They say the place is infested with bats. In the garden, a statue of a knight looms over barbeque grills. Adding to the Goth-frat atmosphere is the stolen gravestone of Elihu Yale, the eighteenth-century merchant that the University is named for, displayed in a glass case in a room with purple walls. A 1980s Bonesman described the Tomb as "a place that used to be really nice but felt kind of beat up, lived in."

The decaying grandeur extends to Deer Island, a Bones-owned island on the St. Lawrence River. Robbins describes the place as follows:

> *The forty-acre retreat is intended to give Bonesmen an opportunity to "get together and rekindle old friendships." A century ago the island sported tennis courts and its softball fields were surrounded by rhubarb plants and gooseberry bushes. Catboats waited on the lake. Stewards catered elegant meals. But although each new Skull and Bones member still visits Deer Island, the place leaves something to be desired. "Now it is just a bunch of burned-out stone buildings," a patriarch sighs. "It's basically ruins." Another Bonesman says that to call the island "rustic" would be to glorify it. "It's a dump, but it's beautiful."* ▲

# THESE BONES GET ALL THE BREAKS

Bonesmen can be found in virtually every sphere of influence, from Wall Street to the White House. Here are some of the especially impressive movers and shakers who were members of the club.

## WILLIAM HOWARD TAFT, CLASS OF 1878

Known as "Big Lub" to his college buddies, he was a shoo-in for Bones since his father co-founded the society. He went on to become the first Bonesman ever to reach The Oval Office.

## AMOS ALONZO STAGG, CLASS OF 1888

Stagg practically invented the modern game of football, but his athletic prowess didn't stop there: To this day, he is the only man to be elected into both the Pro Football Hall of Fame and the Basketball Hall of Fame.

## HENRY SLOANE COFFIN, CLASS OF 1897

His morbid name may have gotten him in the door, but in a club full of WASPs, this guy rose to the top by becoming leader of the Presbyterian Church.

## PERCY ROCKEFELLER, CLASS OF 1900

Naturally, one of the most powerful families in the US would contain at least one Bonesman: Percy went on to be a New York lawyer, oil man, and gun dealer.

## PRESCOTT BUSH, CLASS OF 1916

Legend has it that before he became a United States senator, Prescott and his Bonesman pals dug up and absconded with the skull of the famous Native American warrior Geronimo.

## H.J. HEINZ II, CLASS OF 1931

Your French fries wouldn't be the same without him. The ketchup heir was also father of a US Senator.

## GEORGE HERBERT WALKER BUSH, CLASS OF 1948

Before he became the leader of the free world (and the second Bonesman to achieve that feat), George H. W. Bush had a distinguished career in government service, including a tenure as Director of the CIA. Who better than a Bonesman to keep national security secrets under wraps?

## WILLIAM F. BUCKLEY, CLASS OF 1950

The highly influential conservative American author and commentator was a stickler for tradition in the Tomb—the day before women were set to be admitted to the club, he obtained a court order to keep out the co-eds, insisting that letting in women would lead to rape.

## FREDERICK W. SMITH, CLASS OF 1966

Bonesmen have the world in the palms of their hands—and this one promises "The World on Time" as the founder, chairman, president, and CEO of FedEx.

## JOHN F. KERRY, CLASS OF 1966

The Massachusetts senator, Secretary of State, and debatably heroic Vietnam War veteran challenged fellow Bonesman George W. Bush with a presidential bid in 2004.

## GEORGE W. BUSH, CLASS OF 1968

He wasn't just a cheerleader at Yale—peppy campus party boy "W" joined the family club and went on to become the third Bonesman to occupy the office of US President.

## PAUL GIAMATTI, CLASS OF 1989

The Academy Award-nominated actor known for playing rather schlubby characters may not seem like your typical Bonesman, but his father was once president of Yale. He showed his high-society roots as part of the cast of *Downton Abbey*. ▲

## THE BULLINGDON CLUB
### EST. 1780 AT OXFORD UNIVERSITY

This highly exclusive all-male drinking club does nothing to dispel the perception of Oxford students as arrogant, over-privileged prats. Besides having the correct breeding, Bullingdon members must have an iron gut. At a boozy annual breakfast, barf bags are distributed to prevent members from having to leave the table to vomit (a club offense). Even more stomach-turning is the Bullingdon tradition of trashing unsuspecting restaurants—smashing china, throwing food, and generally leaving the places in ruins. The wealthy and well-connected club members always pay for the damage, but they are unapologetic about their destructive antics. A great number of British aristocrats have participated in these traditions, including Prime Minister David Cameron and London mayor Boris Johnson. A 2014 movie about Bullingdon called *The Riot Club* has university officials concerned about their reputation.

## THE CADAVER SOCIETY
### EST. 1957 AT WASHINGTON AND LEE UNIVERSITY

It's said that two can keep a secret if one of them is dead—but the members of the Cadaver Society have succeeded in keeping their club very hush-hush. The group is thought to be made up of mostly pre-med students, which may account for their namesake. When playing nocturnal pranks, they wear black capes to conceal their identities, and they leave their ominous mark—a letter "C" with a skull inside—around campus. But on the lighter side, the Cadavers contribute great sums of money to the university, which has gone toward scholarships and campus improvements, including a bridge named after their club.

## THE FLAT HAT CLUB
### EST. 1750 AT THE COLLEGE OF WILLIAM & MARY

Formally known as The FHC Society, America's first collegiate secret society is so old that America wasn't even a country when it began. The initials FHC probably stood for something in Latin, but whatever it was has been lost to the ages in favor of the more humorous "Flat Hat Club." The hats in question were the mortarboards worn by William & Mary students in the 18th century (the ones we only have to wear on graduation day now). Founding father Thomas Jefferson was one of the club's early members. He recalled:

> When I was a student of Wm. & Mary college of this state, there existed a society called the F.H.C. society, confined to the number of six students only, of which I was a member, but it had no useful object, nor do I know whether it now exists.

Either Jefferson's time in the FHC was not particularly memorable, or he was just being very guarded with the society's secrets.

## THE HOT FOOT SOCIETY
### EST. 1902 AT UNIVERSITY OF VIRGINIA

The time: Mardi Gras, 1902. The place: the campus of the University of Virginia. Whereas festivals of merriment and excess were already not uncommon on college campuses on the occasion of Fat Tuesday, the Hot Feet went furthest and partied hardest. Their ritualized events (soon to become hallowed traditions within the society) even culminated with the election of a "king."

It didn't take long for the Hot Foot Society to gain a bit of a reputation — which is saying something, especially considering the antics of the University of Virginia's other secret societies of the time, whose signs and symbols could be found scrawled across campus buildings on many occasions. But in 1911, the Hot Feet took things just a bit too far. After a night of presumably heavy drinking, club members went on a vandalism spree, "redecorating" school classrooms and stealing a chamber pot , which was repurposed as the club's ceremonial stein. The administration was none too pleased with this wild escapade, and they came back with the following statement:

> The Hot Foot Society has been, on the whole, very detrimental to the University's welfare, and it is, therefore, unanimously resolved that the existence of the Hot Foot Society, and of all other organizations which promote disorder in the University, shall be forbidden.

With the demise of the Hot Feet, some former members went on to form the IMP Society in 1913, an organization dedicated to preserving the activities they'd come to enjoy, but in slightly more subdued fashion. The IMP Society's mission involves "spreading revelry around Grounds through recognition events of students and faculty, annual community service grants, and other fellowship initiatives." The IMPs also took the lead in welcoming women and blacks to join their club when other clubs at the university kept them out.

## THE IVY CLUB
### EST. 1879 AT PRINCETON UNIVERSITY

The Ivy isn't a secret society but the first of Princeton's many eating clubs. If these clubs were too clandestine, there would be a lot of hungry students on campus, as the majority of upperclassmen take their meals at such establishments to this day.

The original eating clubs came about quite organically, as the student population (and its appetite) grew to a size that the university simply could not accommodate in the dining hall. Students naturally looked to off-campus options for their meals and found a number of boardinghouses that were eager for their business. These meals became social occasions, and the students began to organize into groups, complete with names and traditions of their own. The Ivy Club was founded in 1879 by a group of upperclassmen interested in an even more formal dining routine. It was eventually incorporated, with the college's permission, and established a permanent residence on Prospect Avenue, where other eating clubs soon set up shop.

All of these various clubs developed distinct group personalities over time. In his first novel, *This Side of Paradise*, Princeton alum Scott Fitzgerald gave a description of some of them:

> *Ivy, detached and breathlessly aristocratic; Cottage, an impressive mélange of brilliant adventurers and well-dressed philanderers; Tiger Inn, broad-shouldered and athletic, vitalized by an honest elaboration of prep-school standards; Cap and Gown, anti-alcoholic, faintly religious and politically powerful; flamboyant Colonial; literary Quadrangle; and the dozen others, varying in age and position.*

So how does one get access to the grub? Some eating clubs handpick new members through "bicker," a multi-night process said to be named for the bickering over which applicants to accept. Some operate on a lottery system. Most members agree that in addition to food, the clubs provide a lot of fun.

## THE ORDER OF GIMGHOUL
### EST. 1889 AT THE UNIVERSITY OF NORTH CAROLINA–CHAPEL HILL

Lots of secret societies have fortress-like headquarters, but this one has an actual castle. Gimghoul Castle, built in 1926 in the woods of Chapel Hill,

*Creepiest building on campus.*

is an appropriate home base for the men in this invite-only society, which has roots that recall a gothic novel. As the story goes, UNC student Peter Dromgoole died in a duel, leaving a bloodstain on a rock in Battle Park. The tale inspired five students to form the Order of Dromgoole in 1889. According to William W. Davies, one of the original founders, the name was quickly changed to Gimghoul because it was in "accord with midnight and graves and weirdness." The order perpetuates the weirdness with rituals like dressing in hoods on Halloween night and appearing in Forest Theatre, a popular place for suicides, carrying candles and chanting.

## ORTHOGONIAN SOCIETY
### EST. 1929 AT WHITTIER COLLEGE

Before he became 37th US President, Richard Nixon was denied admittance to Whittier's elite Franklin Club. Not one to be easily defeated, the scrappy freshman brushed off the rejection and helped form the Orthogonians, which means "Square Shooters"—a club for working-class students. The group was founded on the principles of striving for excellence and staying true to oneself, performs community service and fundraising, and produces many student and athletic leaders.

## THE PORCELLIAN CLUB
### EST. 1791 AT HARVARD UNIVERSITY

"The Porc" is Harvard's premier finals club, open only to men. Women can't even cross the threshold of their clubhouse, which is filled with pig memorabilia such as mounted wild boar's heads and a library full of books about pigs. Potential members are evaluated during "punches": elegant weekend outings involving football, drinking, skeet-shooting, and other leisurely pursuits, often on the estate of a wealthy alumnus of the club. And there's no shortage of wealthy alum—Theodore Roosevelt was a member, as were twins Cameron and Tyler Winklevoss, who sued Mark Zuckerberg for stealing their idea for Facebook (the Porc makes a cameo appearance in *The Social Network*, the movie detailing this drama). Wealth and breeding still figure in to eligibility for the club, but for those less fortunate members, it is rumored that the Porcellian presents all members who have not yet achieved economic success by age 30 with an expensive birthday gift—a cool one million dollars.

## QUILL AND DAGGER
### EST. 1893 AT CORNELL UNIVERSITY

Ever hear that old phrase "the pen is mightier than the sword"? Well, put 'em together and you've got a secret society mighty enough to last over a century. Quill and Dagger is a highly prestigious honors society granting membership only to Cornell's best and brightest. It was the first Ivy League secret society to offer membership to women. Members, who meet in the society's elegant tower on campus, are so close they allegedly call each other "soulmates." Along with their rival secret society, Sphinx Head, Quill and Dagger is dedicated to quietly improving Cornell through community service, erecting memorials on campus, and contributing to university traditions (for example, a Quill and Dagger member wrote the Cornell fight song). Many buildings on Cornell's campus are named after prominent alumni of Quill and Dagger.

## TRUST OF THE PEARL
### EST. ? AT UNIVERSITY OF GEORGIA

Entrance into the ranks of this very secret society is considered the highest honor a UGA sorority sister can attain. If you happen to see a woman in black wearing a strand of pearls on campus, it just might be one of the members, though that list is very small—only five are inducted each spring. To determine whom the inductees will be, it is said that current members perform a rite that involves singing, dancing, and tossing pearls in a fire. The new members' faces are then revealed in the flames. ▲

*Death: the party years.*

# LA SANTA MUERTE

FOUNDED: *In Mexico, personifications of Death have existed since the time of the Aztecs, but veneration of Santa Muerte was popularized in the mid-twentieth century.*

STATUS: *More active now than ever before.*

EXCLUSIVITY FACTOR: *Anyone can turn to La Santa Muerte for help or protection—if they are willing to make sacrifices to please her.*

SECRECY FACTOR: *Low. There are shrines to La Santa Muerte in public places all over Mexico.*

THREAT FACTOR: *High. Some members of the cult sacrifice humans so that Santa Muerte will answer their prayers.*

QUIRK FACTOR: *Mexican folk art has some kitsch currency, and the image of Santa Muerte is prime fodder for T-shirts and tattoos.*

## HISTORY AND BACKGROUND

Her name means "Saint Death," and she looks like a grim reaper in fancy dress. Why are so many Mexicans drawn to this ominous figure? Mexicans who practice Catholicism (the country's predominant religion) have always venerated a plurality of saints, the most important being the Virgin Guadalupe. Santa Muerte is sort of like Guadalupe's bad-girl counterpart. One might pray to Guadalupe for blessings like health and happiness; but if you need someone cursed, or even killed, Santa Muerte is the lady to turn to.

Because of her vengeful badass reputation, Santa Muerte attracts a large criminal element. As narcotráfico—drug traffic—has increased in recent years, so has the popularity of Santa Muerte. She, along with a few other figures, is known as a "narco-saint," whom members of Mexico's thriving drug cartels call on for protection and assistance, sometimes even paying tribute with human sacrifice. Members of these cartels live brutal, often short lives, and can relate to this dark deity. Santa Muerte worship has spread like wildfire in Mexican prisons.

In the past decade alone, drug-related violence in Mexico has claimed hundreds of thousands of lives, including many innocent civilians. In the areas where the cartels are most active, people are exposed to unspeakably awful things. The drug lords earn respect through fear by disfiguring their victims and publicly displaying their corpses. Many people who face these horrors on a daily basis have lost hope in the help of traditional deities such as Jesus and the Virgin Guadalupe—but they trust in Santa Muerte to protect them.

This phenomenon has caused great alarm among officials of the Catholic Church, who believe that the proliferation of the cult is the work of Satan. Mexican priests are performing more exorcisms than ever before—but the cult of Santa Muerte shows no signs of dying.

# MEMBERSHIP REQUIREMENTS

Drug lords and gang members are not the only devotees to Santa Muerte. Most others in the cult are poor and live in extremely volatile circumstances. The economic meltdown of the 1990s made many Mexicans turn to any source they could find for help, and Santa Muerte is a "saint of last resort." It is estimated that her cult has about eight million followers in Mexico, with more among Mexican migrants in Central America, the US, and Canada.

To earn the favor of Santa Muerte, one must leave a sacrifice at one of the many shrines devoted to her. It could be something as simple as a white flower—or, for sizable requests, a much more gruesome offering may be required. Human heads have been found at Santa Muerte altars, and it is rumored that some members practice "blood baptism" by wearing the skin of their sacrificial victims.

## INSIDE LA SANTA MUERTE

Santa Muerte is not a fully developed religion, and many practice it in conjunction with Catholicism. It used to be practiced clandestinely through worship at shrines in private homes, but in recent years the cult has become more visible. There are shrines on street corners, temples, and self-proclaimed priests devoted to Santa Muerte.

The image of Santa Muerte is a skeleton holding a scythe draped in long robes. Worshippers may blow smoke, spit alcoholic drinks, or smear narcotics on a statue of the deity to help activate its powers. And the blood and body parts of humans and animals are used in more extreme rituals. Blood may be smeared on devotees, as well as the statue of Santa Muerte.

All of this is done in the hopes that Santa Muerte will perform miracles for her faithful followers. Gang members may pray to her for money or to avoid arrest. However, debts must be settled for answered prayers. One who does not pay proper tribute to Santa Muerte may end up with his head on her altar. ▲

# KILLER CULTS!

Some cults make murder a part of their game. Here are a few notable ones.

## THE MANSON FAMILY

With his wild-eyed stare, delusions of grandeur, and killer instincts, Charles Manson is a psychopath through and through. This maniac and his merry band terrorized California during the tumultuous summer of 1969.

Young Charlie was a juvenile delinquent-turned-career criminal who had spent more than half of his life locked up in jail before landing in San Francisco in the Summer of Love, 1967. He established himself as a guru in the hippie-infested Haight-Asbury district, where he found many (mostly female) followers. He preached a philosophy derived partly from Scientology, which he had studied in prison. He also encouraged free love, and he and all of his followers lived together as "The Manson Family." It's a testament to Manson's animal magnetism that he convinced a bunch of his followers to travel with him to Los Angeles, where they settled down with some new converts they had picked up along the way.

For a few months, the Family commandeered the Hollywood home of Beach Boy Dennis Wilson, who had befriended Manson and tried to help him achieve his dream of becoming a rock star. But the guru's musical talent was lacking, and his entourage of miscreants didn't make the best houseguests. After being kicked out of Wilson's home in 1968, Manson relocated the Family to the Spahn's Movie Ranch, an out-of-use set for Western productions.

It was there that the Manson Family's story turned into a horror movie. Manson became obsessed with the Beatles' White Album and claimed that the music was speaking to him in code. He predicted there would be a race war in the summer of 1969—a time of chaos he called "Helter Skelter," after a song on the album. He directed his drug-fueled followers to strike out.

The first to die at the hands of the Manson Family was Gary Hinman, an associate of one of the men in the Family who had allegedly been involved in a drug deal gone bad. They held Hinman hostage for two days in July 1969 before stabbing him to death.

In August, Manson dispatched four of his followers to 10050 Cielo Drive, the home of movie director Roman Polanski. He wasn't home, but others were: Polanski's wife, actress Sharon Tate, who was eight and a half months pregnant; her friend Jay Sebring, a celebrity hairstylist; Polanski's friend, writer Wojciech Frykowski; Frykowski's lover Abigail Folger, heiress to the Folger coffee fortune; and 18-year-old student Steven Parent, who had the misfortune of going to visit his friend, a groundskeeper on the property, on that fateful night. Parent was shot in the driveway, before Manson's crew cut the phone lines and sneaked into the house to continue their killing spree. With knives and guns, they slaughtered everyone inside. Sharon Tate begged for the life of her unborn baby, but she was mercilessly stabbed to death despite her pleas.

Manson was displeased at how the messy massacre went down, so the next night, he set off from the Spahn Ranch with six of his followers to show them how it was done. They ended up at the home of supermarket executive Leno LaBianca and his wife, Rosemary. The Family woke the sleeping couple and killed them in a stabbing frenzy.

These murders rocked Los Angeles, but it wasn't until October that police figured out that the murders may have been related. Graffiti, written in blood at the crime scenes, provided the link. The writings were all Beatles references, saying things like "Death to pigs" and "Healter [sic] Skelter." Manson and the people who had killed for him were finally arrested.

The 1970 trial was a circus, with Manson making outrageous statements ("Why blame it on me? I didn't write the music!") and doing things like carving an "X" into his forehead for attention. The women on trial, still loyal to Charlie, followed his lead and carved X's into their own foreheads. Even Manson Family members who were not locked up did the same. Jurors were horrified by the distasteful performance of these seemingly unrepentant murderers.

Manson and his followers were found guilty and sentenced to death, but their sentences were automatically reduced to life in prison in 1972 when the

California Supreme Court abolished the death penalty in that state. Charles Manson remains incarcerated at California's Corcoran State Prison, but even from there he retains a hold over the imaginations of many who find his story morbidly fascinating.

## AUM SHINRIKYO/ALEPH

It's hard to believe that what began as a yoga and meditation group evolved to biological warfare, but that is exactly what happened with Japan's Aum Shinrikyo. The group's founder and spiritual leader, Shoko Asahara, has claimed to be the first "enlightened one" since Buddha, capable of levitation and mind-reading. This fatherly guru took in thousands of young Japanese who were seeking a more meaningful existence. He insisted that the apocalypse was nigh, though the dates were a little unclear—the end would come either in 1996, or between 1999 and 2003.

Clearly Asahara's predictions did not prove true, but when he started a yoga school in his one-room apartment in 1984, those dates were still far in the future. He taught his devoted followers psychic-development exercises to aid in their growth and enlightenment. By the time he became interested in prophecy, Aum Shinrikyo was designated as an official religious organization. According to Asahara, only Aum members would survive the coming apocalypse, after which the group would take the place of the Japanese government.

The end, he said, would be hastened by the US starting World War III with Japan. Because of this, Aum had to be armed and ready to fight. Brilliant young scientists were recruited from top universities to aid the group in this respect. In secret laboratories near Mount Fuji, they produced an arsenal of biochemical weapons, including nerve agents such as VX and killer diseases such as anthrax and Q-fever. The cult also established its own militia.

Armed with chemical agents, this violent group began taking out their "enemies" left and right, incinerating some victims in specially built microwave ovens in their laboratories near Mount Fuji. Then, in 1994, Aum conducted a sarin gas attack in Matsumoto city. The targets of the deadly attack were three judges presiding over a case against Aum—but the nerve gas killed seven people and injured two hundred others. Tragically, the authorities did not connect Aum to the attack until the group committed their most infamous deed: the Tokyo subway attack.

The increasingly paranoid Asahara responded to a police investigation of the cult by orchestrating a Sarin gas attack on the Tokyo subway in 1995. Twelve people were killed and over five thousand injured in that horrific rush hour raid. If the cult members who carried out the attack hadn't experienced technical difficulties with their distribution system, they could have killed tens of thousands of commuters. In the aftermath of this atrocity, they committed several smaller scale attacks throughout Tokyo, with varying degrees of success, until finally Asahara and several other senior Aum members were arrested.

Asahara was jailed and sentenced to death (in 2012, his execution was postponed). But outside of his prison, Aum Shinrikyo still survives. The group reformed in 2000, changing their name to Aleph. They have not committed any acts of terrorism since 1995, but plenty of devotees still believe in Asahara's twisted teachings.

# LINEAMIENTO UNIVERSAL SUPERIOR (LUS—SUPERIOR UNIVERSAL ALIGNMENT)

Were you born after 1981? If so, you'd better stay away from the LUS sect. These South American kooks consider children to be evil, especially if they were born after that year.

In 1981, their leader, Valentina de Andrade, began spreading the message she claimed was passed on to her by cosmic beings: that God does not exist, Jesus is an extraterrestrial, and only members of her group would survive the pending destruction of the Earth by escaping in a spacecraft. She established Lineamiento Universal Superior, LUS, to fulfill her mission. To join LUS, members abandoned their children, who de Andrade considered to be "negative energies." Her followers would be ready for a fresh start once the UFO promised by de Andrade came for them.

But there were dark dealings to contend with on earth first. From 1989 to 1993 in Altamira in northern Brazil's Para state, nineteen children were abducted and suffered mutilation and torture at the hands of LUS Boys ages 8 to 13 were castrated, supposedly as part of a black magic ritual, and then left for dead in the woods. The community was shocked by these gruesome crimes, but for a time they went unsolved.

Then in 1992, de Andrade and her group were investigated in connection with the disappearance of a child on the Brazilian island of Guaratuba. They avoided prosecution when witness accounts were inconsistent—possibly the result of intimidation and influence-peddling, which de Andrade and her accomplices used to avoid prosecution for many years.

Valentina de Andrade fled for Argentina. In the meantime, authorities gathered enough evidence to bring four LUS members to trial for their roles in the killings. Two of the men convicted and sentenced to prison were the physicians who performed the castrations.

Five children survived the tortures of LUS Two of them testified at the trial of Valentina de Andrade, which did not take place until 2003. One young man recounted in graphic detail his abduction, being put to sleep with a foul-smelling rag held over his face, and how he awoke in a wooded area, naked and missing his genitals. But incredibly, even with this testimony, de Andrade was acquitted. If she ever does make her great escape to space, this evil woman will not be missed. ▲

The Thule Society's emblem
did not improve with age.

# THE THULE SOCIETY

FOUNDED: *1918*

STATUS: *Dissolved around 1926; revived with rise of Nazism in 1933, but died out again soon after.*

EXCLUSIVITY FACTOR: *Only the whitest of the white were admitted. Initiates were required to submit a photograph as proof of "purity of race" and make a "blood declaration" that "no Jewish or coloured blood runs through his veins."*

SECRECY FACTOR: *They held public lectures on German history, but outsiders were not aware of what went on at their members-only meetings.*

THREAT FACTOR: *High. This organization might have planted the seeds of Nazism.*

QUIRK FACTOR: *The society has been depicted in many comics, novels, and movies as the occult force behind the Nazi regime.*

## HISTORY AND BACKGROUND

Many famous people have been involved with secret societies. One of the 20th century's most infamous villains, Adolph Hitler, may have been connected to this one. The Thule Society was a German occultist study group in Munich. They were named for the legendary lost continent of Thule, believed to be the home of the Aryan race. Members of the Thule Society thought that through magical rituals, they could access the otherworldly powers of this ancient "master race," enabling Germany to dominate the world.

The Thule society was one of many groups in this period that were part of the völkisch movement. The word völkisch has no direct English translation, but it roughly means "nationalist" or "populist." Völkisch groups essentially believed humans to be pre-formed by inherited characteristics—race being the most obvious. The völkisch school of thought also included anti-Semitic, anti-communist, anti-immigration, anti-capitalist, and anti-Parliamentarian principles. These ideas were very influential on Hitler when he took over the National Socialist, or Nazi party. Once he had control of Germany, most völkisch groups became absorbed by the Nazis, or else declared heretical.

But before Hitler came on the scene, the most prominent figure of German anti-Semitism was a man named Theodor Fritsch. He was the founder of a group called the Germanenorden (Germanic or Teutonic Order), a völkisch secret society formed in Munich in 1912. Fritsch believed there was a Jewish plot to take over Germany's economy, and with the Germanenorden he hoped to bring together anti-Semites like himself to fight "the Jewish Menace." The order was modeled on the Freemasonry, with similar rituals, secret passwords, and handshakes. Their symbol was a swastika, long before it was co-opted by the Nazis. The Germanenorden claimed that marriage between Germans and Jews cut off Aryans from their racial memory and innate psychic powers. But not many Germans at the time were into these crank theories—even the chapter in Nuremburg, Bavaria's hub of anti-Jewish sentiment, had less than fifty members.

The Germanenorden limped along until 1917, until a Munich-based man called Rudolf Freiherr von Sebottendorf came across one of their advertisements in a right-wing newspaper inviting "German-blooded, serious men of pure character" to join a "Germanic lodge." Sebottendorf was a wealthy adventurer with an interest in the occult—he practiced meditation, astrology, numerology, and alchemy. He was also a Freemason, so it wasn't a stretch for him to become a part of the copycat Germanenorden. He traveled to Munich to be initiated, and then continued on to recruit for the order. Sebottendorf lectured, wrote magazine articles, and subsidized a newsletter out of his own pocket, all to promote "Deutschland den Deutschen"—"Germany for the

Germans"—excluding Jews, of course. The country was going through tough times, with having been defeated in the First World War in 1918, so more folks were receptive to the message.

Sebottendorf allied with a young member of the order, Walter Nauhaus, a Munich art student and one of many disgruntled veterans wounded in the war. Nauhaus was head of another Germanic study group called the Thule Gesellschaft. He recruited young members, while Sebottendorf worked on the older ones. They signed up 1,500 new Germanenorden members in the province of Bavaria by 1919.

The study of German Antiquity was all well and good, but since the German Revolution (a conflict that resulted in the replacement of Germany's imperial government with a republic, with a brief period of communism in between) was taking place in 1918–1919, Sebottendorf was interested in transitioning the Germanenorden to political action. In July 1918, Thule Gesellschaft merged with Germanenorden to become the Thule Society, a group with a more racist and anti-Semitic rhetoric than its predecessors, dedicated to combating "the Jewish-Bolshevik terror."

# MEMBERSHIP REQUIREMENTS

First and foremost, members of the Thule society had to be of Aryan descent. How was such a thing proven in the days before DNA testing? Those wishing to join had to submit a photograph, which was examined for purity of race. They were also required to make the following "blood declaration":

> *The signer hereby swears to the best of his knowledge and belief that no Jewish or coloured blood flows in either his or in his wife's veins, and that among their ancestors are no members of the colored races.*

The people who made the cut were affluent, influential people from Munich society: professors, noblemen, manufacturers, senior officials, business people—including a who's who of Nazi sympathizers. Members of the

*The monster who needs no introduction.*

Thule Society were among the first people who allied themselves with Hitler. Key members of the Nazi party including Rudolf Hess, Alfred Rosenberg, Hans Frank, Julius Lehmann, Gottfried Feder, Dietrich Eckart, and Karl Harrer were allegedly Thule members, though some may have just visited as speakers. Hitler, too, may have spoken at a meeting, but there's no evidence that he was actually a member. Even for the engineers of a genocide, involvement with a racist organization such as Thule wasn't something to advertise.

In 1933, Rudolf Freiherr von Sebottendorf, the combined group's erstwhile leader, published a book called *Before Hitler Came: Documents from the Early Days of the National Socialist Movement*, dealing with the Thule Society's role in the evolution of the Nazi party. The Führer didn't appreciate this exposé, which he felt to be exploitative and inaccurate, and the book was banned. Sebottendorf was imprisoned, but somehow escaped—probably with help from one of his high-powered Munich cronies—and fled to Turkey. Interestingly, he may have worked as a double agent for both Germany and the Allies during World War II. Sebottendorf committed suicide by jumping into the Turkish strait the Bosphorus in 1945.

## INSIDE THE THULE SOCIETY

The Thule Society held its meetings at the elegant Four Seasons Hotel in Munich, conducting an official dedication ceremony on August 17, 1918. The group no longer had time for occult nonsense (such as the divining rods that Sebottendorf sometimes played around with) and concentrated on more serious political goals. The members discussed staging a coup and quietly built a cache of weapons. They welcomed other nationalist groups in their rooms, their allies in planning a counterrevolution.

Together these groups recruited and provided funding for the freikorps (free corps), a paramilitary group that fought against the communists (and would provide the basis for Hitler's Sturmabteilung storm troopers). Sebottendorf wasn't afraid to get his own hands dirty—in December 1918, he attempted to assassinate Kurt Eisner, then the premier of Bavaria. Sebottendorf failed, but someone else succeeded in February 1919. After Eisner's demise, the communists so despised by the Thule Society seized control of Munich, creating the short-lived Bavarian Soviet Republic.

The communists threatened to take hostages, and made good on that threat when they raided the Thule Society's headquarters in April 1919. They captured the secretary, Countess Heila von Westarp, and six other Thule members on the basis of their counterrevolutionary criminal activity. The Thule gang and a few other prisoners were executed, enraging the popu-lace. There was an uprising in Munich, with Thule participating, and by early May, anti-communist forces (including the German Army and the freikorps funded by Thule) defeated the Bolsheviks.

The Thule Society and its racist friends used the actions of the Jewish leadership in the establishment of the Bavarian Soviet Republic to attack the greater German Jewish community. In 1918, Sebottendorf bought a news-paper called *Völkischer Beobachter* (*Völkisch Observer*), in which he ran anti-Semitic rants and notices about meetings of various völkisch groups. In October 1919, the paper covered a meeting of the Deutsche Arbeiterpartei (DAP), the German Worker's Party. It mentioned one member, "Herr Hitler," speaking passionately at the meeting of a need for a union against Jews. His special brand of delivery of this racist rhetoric would take him far, though nobody knew just how far yet.

The DAP, the entity that put power behind Hitler's voice, was itself an offshoot of the Thule Society. To stand up against the Reds and the

"Jewish Menace," the Thule realized they had to expand beyond their aristocratic base. Society member Karl Harrer, in conjunction with a locksmith named Anton Drexler, organized a workman's discussion group in October, 1918. This group became the DAP, and the DAP would eventually become the National Socialist Party—the Nazis. Hitler purchased the *Völkischer Beobachter* newspaper from Sebottendorf and used it as his own platform for spreading Nazi propaganda.

In the wake of the hostage crisis, tensions in the Thule Society caused schisms in the group, and it eventually died out around 1926. When Hitler came to power in 1933, the Thule Society was briefly revived, again holding meetings at the Four Seasons Hotel in Munich, but this time around, it was a more purely social affair. Some diehard old members who showed up for the racism and magic were unhappy with this new direction, and once more the society split and foundered. Eventually, under the Nazi regime, secret societies were banned—some Freemasons were even thrown in concentration camps. Hitler did not want to be associated with groups such as Thule, but the fact remains that they were key players in the dictator's rise to power. ▲

# THE FÜHRER'S FLYING SAUCERS

After World War II ended, it was revealed that the Germans had been working on some secret weapons so powerful they might have changed the course of the war. One project in development was the Messerschmidt 264 bomber, also known by the frightening moniker the "Amerikabomber," which Hitler had planned to use to blow up New York City. Luckily, Germany was defeated before this plan could come to fruition. But did the Nazis succeed in mastering more otherworldly technology?

According to myth, in 1937, an alien craft crashed in the German countryside. The army gathered the remains of the spaceship—there is no record of whether any bodies were retrieved. Hitler always had an interest in the occult, so he must have been very excited by this occurrence. He had the remains of the craft put in a warehouse, which was guarded around the clock, and enlisted the country's top aeronautical experts to sift through the wreckage. A team was assembled to reverse-engineer a flying disc like the one that was salvaged.

One of the developers was a German aircraft designer named Rudolf Schriever, who worked on several disc-shaped aircrafts. He led construction of a circular air vehicle 137 feet in diameter with an elongated hump on top for the cockpit. This prototype, housed in a facility in Poland, was deliberately destroyed by the retreating German troops before it could be overtaken by the Soviets in 1945.

But Schriever had another secret lair just outside Prague where another disc aircraft was supposedly under construction. Diagrams from Rudolf Lusar's influential book German Secret Weapons of the Second World War show a futuristic machine (complete with an egg-shaped cockpit) that appears to rely on a combination of fan blades and jet engines in order to achieve flight. When it was tested, the machine was rumored to have reached an altitude of 39,000 feet in just over three minutes, and had the capability to move faster than the speed of sound, which seems much too incredible to be true. As with most of the pieces of this Nazi UFO mythology, the authenticity of these reports is suspect—but then again, would a government admit to building machines modeled on a crashed alien spaceship?

Another guy handpicked by Hitler to take a stab at zero-gravity technology was an oddball named Viktor Schauberger, who had previously worked as a forester and considered the natural world his greatest teacher. Many considered his unorthodox approach to engineering to be a bit nutty. Schauberger didn't seem to have any problem with that, saying: "They call me deranged. The hope is they are right." Perhaps only a deranged mind could create a Nazi superweapon!

Attempting to work with nature instead of against it, Schauberger created a flying saucer that used a "vortex propulsion" system—oscillating water or air until it gathered enough energy to cause levitation. He built several models—at least one was constructed using prison labor at the Mauthausen concentration camp—and apparently one actually flew. But the machine was destroyed by the Nazis at the end of the war before it could be seized by the Allies.

If these mysterious flying saucers did exist, few people saw them—Schrieber's machines were even alleged to have killed two test pilots. But many Allied pilots claimed to have spotted other aircrafts they suspected to be created by the Germans: flying balls of fire they called "foo fighters." These were thought to be small remote-controlled aircraft armed with devices to interfere with the electronics and engines of the planes they followed. The pilots who encountered the foo fighters described them as fast-moving, round, glowing objects that made wild maneuvers in the sky, and could seemingly not be shot down. However, since these pilots lived to tell the tale, it doesn't seem that their engines were interfered with, as the craft were purportedly made to do. The generally accepted theory is that the "foo fighters" the pilots saw were just some innocent natural phenomenon.

With so much evidence of these top-secret projects allegedly destroyed, it's nearly impossible to verify any of these stories. But there are some people who believe that the Nazi flying saucers were not actually wiped out—that when Germany was defeated, the Allies found the plans for the aircraft and used them to build their own versions. Test runs of those machines could account for the UFOs sightings in America and Russia during the 1950s. Or maybe the original Nazi flying saucers could have strayed and are still cruising around today, with a crew of extraterrestrial SS officers inside. ▲

*Workin' on their knight moves.*

# THE SOCIETY FOR CREATIVE ANACHRONISM

FOUNDED: *1966*

STATUS: *Active*

EXCLUSIVITY FACTOR: *All good ladies and gentles are welcome!*

SECRECY FACTOR: *To an outsider, it's deeply curious; to an insider, it's pleyn as dai.*

THREAT FACTOR: *Low—those aren't real swords.*

QUIRK FACTOR: *High—verily, it is so.*

## HISTORY AND BACKGROUND

The Middle Ages was a fascinating time, rich with history, women in corsets, and men in tights. While most people can get their olde-tymey fix by taking in a joust at the local Renaissance Faire, those seeking a more immersive experience can join the Society for Creative Anachronism (SCA): an international organization dedicated to researching and recreating the arts and skills of pre-17th-century Europe.

You may have seen people in makeshift armor sparring with wooden swords in a park or college campus and wondered what the heck they were doing. This hearkens back to the beginnings of the SCA—to Berkeley, California, in 1966, when a few friends hosted an outdoor party featuring a jousting tournament. The invitation summoned "all knights to defend in single combat the title of 'fairest' for their ladies." The event was a great success, and word spread throughout the community of science fiction and fantasy fans, who organized bigger events and local "kingdoms." Today, there are over thirty thousand members all over the world. The founding of the SCA is also considered to be the beginning of fantasy LARPing (live action role playing).

But it's not all about jousting. As the group's name suggests, SCA members practice all kinds of creatively anachronistic ("out of time") pursuits including archery, equestrian activities, costuming, cooking, herbalism, metalwork, woodworking, music, dance, calligraphy, needlework, and much more. The group boasts: "If it was done in the Middle Ages or Renaissance, odds are you'll find someone in the SCA interested in recreating it."

However, there are some parts of the era that the SCA is not interested in reviving. There's no serf class or bubonic plague or horrifying torture devices. Their version of the Dark Ages is, in a word, much brighter—with electric lights and heated halls used at society gatherings, and indoor plumbing fortunately replacing chamber pots. With an emphasis on chivalry and art, medieval groupies continue to delight in the SCA's version of "the current middle ages."

## MEMBERSHIP REQUIREMENTS

Anyone with an interest in the Middle Ages can join the SCA—and if you know how to play a lute, so much the better. Even teenagers can participate, and there are often whole families involved in the feudal fun. The first step toward joining is to locate your local kingdom. The SCA's "Knowne World" (a reference to maps of the time, which were for the most part limited to the areas that explorers had actually visited) consists of nineteen kingdoms divided by geographic region, all over the world. These large kingdoms are broken down into Principalities and local chapters called Baronies, Shires, and Cantons, each with its own board of officers to run it. Within some of these chapters are unofficial groups called Households and Guilds focused on specific interests within the era.

Next, you've got to pick a name for yourself. It could be something simple based on your location (Mary of London) or vocation (Thomas the Smith); something based on personality (Aidan the Hostile) or physical traits (Jason the Tall); or something utterly unpronounceable (UlfR Blodfotur Fallgrson).

However, no one may use the name of an actual person from history or legend, and titles such as Sir, Lord, Lady, Earl, Duke, Count, Master, or Mistress must be earned. Unlike medieval Europe, the class system within the SCA is merit-based. For their hard work, special skills, and other contributions to the group, members are rewarded by moving up through the ranks of nobility. Many members go beyond just a name and create a whole new persona of who they might have been in the Middle Ages, and they stay in character at SCA events.

## INSIDE THE SCA

Once you are a member, you can attend events like feasts, tournaments, coronations, masked balls, inter-kingdom wars, and more—but you must come in costume. If you've ever wanted to don a wimple or chainmail, this is the place to do it. Ready-to-wear medieval garb can be expensive, so you may choose to go the DIY route. Other society members will probably be happy to teach you to make period clothing, and you don't have to worry about the drudgery of period sewing methods—modern sewing machines are permitted.

But if you're looking for action on the battlefield, becoming authorized to fight in the SCA takes a bit more time. Wannabe warriors craft their own armor from steel, rivets, leather, even well-disguised plastic. Swords are made from rattan, a material similar to bamboo. Experienced fighters teach novices how to use their weapons, how to defend themselves, and how to judge blows received in combat. Safety officers called marshals then grant authorization to fight. Once authorized, combatants face off in single combat tournaments, or in large melee battles.

Veteran members will also guide you in the etiquette and jargon used by the group and can help you with any other special skills you may want to learn—falconry, anyone? Being an outstanding member of the SCA requires real dedication, but it may just be the next best thing to traveling back in time. ▲

*For more information, visit their wildly anachronistic website at www.sca.org.*

# THE ROYAL TREATMENT

What's it like to be a monarch in the SCA? Here's what rulers of various kingdoms in the "Knowne World" have to say.

**What is the proper form of address for royalty?**

In the SCA, kings and queens are addressed as "Your Majesty." That's not, however, a historically accurate term. In the Middle Ages, royalty was addressed as "Your Grace." That's just one of the anachronisms that are part of the Society for Creative Anachronism.

*—Sir Guillaume de la Belgique, former ruler of Caid*

**Is it better to rule by love or by fear?**

Without a doubt, the answer to that is love. Inside many of the crowns that are worn by monarchs in the SCA, there is an inscription that says, "You rule because they believe." Not a truer statement could be said. At the heart of it, the Crown's job is to lead and to recognize the efforts of the citizens of their Kingdom. Without the love of your populace, your reign is just an empty shell.

*—King Ulrich of Meridies*

**In the Middle Ages, kings and queens were granted sovereignty by divine right. How are they appointed in the SCA?**

In many ways, the SCA is based more on the legends of King Arthur than on the history of the Middle Ages. Just as King Arthur drew a sword from a stone at a tournament, in the SCA, we hold tournaments to select our monarchs. Periodically (twice a year in most kingdoms) a Crown Tournament is held, where all the warriors of the kingdom don their armor and compete with their swords to determine the champion. The winner of the day will rule as king (or queen!) for the term of the next reign. And, just like the legend of the sword in the stone, anyone—from the youngest warrior to the most experienced veteran—can be victorious in Crown Tournament.

You don't need to be from a royal family to take the throne.

— *Sir Guillaume de la Belgique, former ruler of Caid*

## What are the duties of a King or Queen in the SCA?

We are the figureheads of the Kingdom, and I see our duties as being good officers of the Kingdom. We are responsible for ensuring that those who deserve it are recognized for duties they perform, work they have done, and skill shown in fighting and the Arts & Sciences. The most important duty of the crown is we are the ones others look to for the fun factor of our game. We are in a sense responsible for everyone having fun.

—*Emperor Krotuas Horatius Caesar Augustus, Trimaris*

## Are your subjects ever unruly?

I have unfortunately had to banish two persons during this reign. Since we do not exclude any persons from the organization, occasionally unhappy souls walk in and cause problems that must sometimes be dealt with.

—*King Obadiah the Obstreperous of Ravenslocke, Kingdom of the West*

## Describe a royal feast. Do you get more food than the average lord or lady?

A royal feast usually consists of three to seven courses, each of which could be a complete meal by itself. No one goes home hungry, and one must pace oneself, or be so full by the end of the second course that the next course is more a trial than a joy. Imagine Thanksgiving dinner. You eat your fill of turkey and stuffing. Then, just as you're wondering if you can even eat another bite of mincemeat pie, someone brings out a complete second dinner of ham and baked potatoes. A royal feast is like that, except that instead of turkey and stuffing you might have capon with mushrooms and leeks, and instead of ham and potatoes it might be venison and frumenty [A dish made primarily from boiled, cracked wheat].

The royalty and the great nobles sit at the head table, with the rest of the populace at a group of lower tables, usually with an open area between for bards and other performers. The head table may get more food, but since even the amount served at the lower tables is more than anyone can eat, it is more for show than a benefit for us.

—*Garick, Rex Outlands*

**What kind of entertainment of the Middle Ages do you most enjoy?**

I enjoy this organization on many levels. I am an artist and enjoy working as such, doing the medieval arts of calligraphy, illumination, silver smithing, glass bead making, coining, cooking, and brewing. There are many other activities as well, with falconers, musicians, and thespians all within the society. The SCA makes a perfect outlet for these skills and hobbies.

—*King Obadiah the Obstreperous of Ravenslocke, Kingdom of the West*

**If you had a castle, what would it be called?**

Actually . . . I do have a castle! It's called Chepstow, and it's in Gloucestershire in England. Several years ago I coordinated a group of SCA members to put on a demonstration of armored sword-fighting inside Chepstow castle for the public. The castle's administration staff enjoyed the demonstration so much that at the end of the day, they presented me with the key to the castle gate.

—*Sir Guillaume de la Belgique, former ruler of Caid*

**Who is the heir to your throne? Are you ever worried he or she might kill you in order to claim it?**

My Prince and Princess are close friends of mine. They have been King and Queen before so they are a big help with Royal duties. In the SCA, when we step down from being the Crown, often it is through roleplay of assassins or death in battle. I do a Roman persona, so when I step down it is my intention to be murdered as Julius Caesar was. Thankfully, it is a mob of my friends and we will all have a great time with it.

—*Emperor Krotuas Horatius Caesar Augustus, Trimaris*

**Who is your favorite real life royal, past or present?**

Eleanor of Aquitaine is one of my favorite royals. And Williams Marshall, though only an Earl, was a true knight. At 65 years of age he was still feared by Kings, and forced John to sign Magna Carta. He served four Kings, for the last, Henry III as his regent. He was one of the most powerful men in Europe at this time—he could have made himself king when he was regent for the young king, but swore to defend and rule for him. Many have called him the flower of chivalry and the greatest knight. Even Richard the Lionheart, known for his prowess, feared Williams.

*—King Obadiah the Obstreperous of Ravenslocke, Kingdom of the West*

**What's the best part of being King?**

Without a doubt, the best part is the opportunity to award people for their good work. The moment of shock and joy as someone kneeling before us in Court realizes that they have been granted titles of nobility is the pinnacle of the royal experience.

*—Garick, Rex Outlands* ▲

# WANTED

## NATIONAL FIREARMS ACT

### William Taylor Harris

Date photographs taken unknown
FBI No.: 308,668 L5
Aliases: Mike Andrews, Richard Frank Dennis, William Kinder, Jonathan Maris, Jonathan Mark Salamone, Teko
Age: 29, born January 22, 1945, Fort Sill, Oklahoma (not supported by birth records)
Height: 5'7"          Eyes: Hazel
Weight: 145 pounds    Complexion: Medium
Build: Medium         Race: White
Hair: Brown, short    Nationality: American
Occupation: Postal clerk
Marks: Reportedly wears Fu Manchu type mustache, may wear glasses, upper right center tooth may be chipped, reportedly jogs, swims and rides bicycle for exercise, was last seen wearing army type boots and dark jacket
Social Security Numbers Used: 315-46-2467; 553-27-8400; 359-48-5467
Fingerprint Classification: 20 I. 1 At 12
                            S  1 Ut

### Emily

Date pho
FBI No.: 3
Aliases: Mrs. William
Joanne James, Anna L
Dorothy Ann Petri, Em
Mary Schwartz, Yoland
Age: 27, born Februar
      (not supported by
Height: 5'3"
Weight: 115 pounds
Build: Small
Hair: Blonde
Occupation: retary
Remarks: may be
wear glasses or contact
upper plate, pierced ear
by jogging, swimming a
slacks or street length
and waist length shiny
Social Security Number

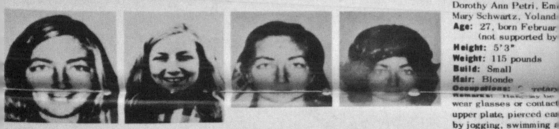

## NATIONAL FIREARMS ACT; BANK ROBBERY

### Patricia Campbell Hearst

FBI No.: 325,805 L10
Alias: Tania
Age: 20, born February 20, 1954, San Francisco, California
Height: 5'3"          Eyes: Brown
Weight: 110 pounds    Complexion: Fair
Build: Small          Race: White
Hair: Light brown     Nationality: American
Scars and Marks: Mole on lower right corner of mouth, scar near right ankle
Remarks: Hair naturally light brown, straight and worn about three inches below shoulders in length, however, may wear wigs, including Afro style, dark brown of medium length; was last seen wearing black sweater, plaid slacks, brown hiking boots and carrying a knife in her belt

Jan., 1971     Feb., 1972     Dec., 19

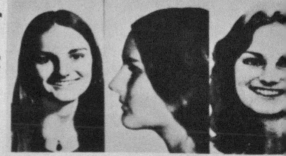

THESE INDIVIDUALS ARE SELF-PROCLAIMED MEMBERS OF THE SYMBIONESE LIBERATION ARMY AND RE
OF VARIOUS FIREARMS INCLUDING AUTOMATIC WEAPONS. WILLIAM HARRIS AND PATRICIA HEARST
THREE SHOULD BE CONSIDERED ARMED AND VERY DANGEROUS.
issued on May 20, 1974, at Los Angeles, California, charging the Harrises and Hearst with violati
also returned by a Federal Grand Jury on June 6, 1974, at San Francisco, California, for bank robbery and us

IF YOU HAVE ANY INFORMATION CONCERNING THESE PERSONS, PLEASE NOTIFY ME OR
OFFICE, THE TELEPHONE NUMBER OF WHICH APPEARS ON THE FIRST PAGE OF MO

# THE SYMBIONESE LIBERATION ARMY

FOUNDED: *1973*

STATUS: *Disbanded in 1975*

EXCLUSIVITY FACTOR: *Militants and heiresses welcome*

SECRECY FACTOR: *Remained underground until its first public act of violence in 1973.*

THREAT FACTOR: *High, especially for those who were part of the capitalist machine.*

QUIRK FACTOR: *Supposed member Patty Hearst went on to act in several campy John Waters films—doesn't get much quirkier than that.*

## HISTORY AND BACKGROUND

It's an iconic image: a young white woman wearing fatigues and a beret, a look of cold determination on her face while brandishing an assault rifle with expert poise. This intimidating figure is newspaper heiress Patty Hearst, and her involvement in the Symbionese Liberation Army remains the group's lasting legacy. Nineteen-year-old Hearst was kidnapped by the SLA in 1974, and during her imprisonment she appeared to have adopted the group's revolutionary politics, renouncing her bourgeois family in recorded statements and participating in criminal activities, including armed robbery. Hearst's kidnapping is widely considered to be a case of Stockholm Syndrome (see page 210).

But who were these "soldiers" who apparently earned the sympathy of the heiress? The SLA was formed in Berkeley, California, in 1973. At that time, many counter cultural adherents had left behind the radical politics of the

1960s—but a few moved from radical, to revolutionary, eschewing the sit-ins and peaceful protests of the previous decade for militant action.

Perhaps the most well-known paramilitary group of this sort was the Black Panthers (see page 211), who espoused communist beliefs and aimed to improve society by combating injustices such as police brutality and racial inequality. Young white radicals took up the Panthers' armed struggle ideology, and Berkeley was inundated with their collectives and communes.

The prison system was a hotbed for the type of institutional violence that these radicals opposed. To help combat this, in the late 1960s, a University of California-Berkeley professor formed an inmate organization called the Black Cultural Association (BCA) to empower inmates through education. The group brought college students to California's Vacaville prison to tutor prisoners in a range of subjects: math, reading, writing, art, history, political science, sociology, and African heritage were all covered. Over time, this association became increasingly political and largely focused on black nationalism. Donald DeFreeze, a black Vacaville prisoner who was involved with the BCA, formed a splinter group that, in 1973, became the SLA.

The group came into being when DeFreeze escaped from prison and reconnected with some of his friends in Berkeley. Together, they formed the Symbionese Liberation Army and appointed DeFreeze (with his new alias, "General Field Marshal Cinque") as their leader. Their goals were manifold, but they included ending racism, monogamy, the prison system, and other institutions that had earned their ire.

The SLA's first act of terrorism occurred on November 6, 1973, when they murdered Oakland School's black superintendent Marcus Foster with cyanide-laced bullets. Their grievance with Foster was that he supported an identification system for students. The country was horrified by this killing, and even Berkeley's most die-hard lefties found the political murder of a black man incomprehensible. The SLA members went into hiding, but when a few were captured and arrested for the Foster murder, others set their safe house on fire to destroy evidence.

Their next target was Patricia Campbell Hearst, heir to the Hearst media fortune. On February 4, 1974, the Berkeley College undergraduate was at home with her fiancé when three members of the SLA forced their way in. After assaulting her fiancé with a wine bottle, they carried Hearst, clothed in a nightgown, out of her apartment and forced her into the trunk of a car.

A media furor erupted over the kidnapping, and the local police and FBI launched a search for the missing woman. Then two days later, the SLA released a communique via a Berkeley radio station in which it called the abduction the "serving of an arrest warrant on Patricia Campbell Hearst." It warned that any attempt to rescue Hearst would result in her execution. The statement ended with the SLA's slogan: "DEATH TO THE FASCIST INSECT THAT PREYS UPON THE LIFE OF THE PEOPLE." It made no demand for ransom.

The Hearst family was unsure how to negotiate with these revolutionaries. In another recording, Patty Hearst assured her parents that she was okay, that she was not being starved or beaten—and she told the police not to try to find her. The package received by the radio station also included the photograph of Hearst brandishing a carbine and wearing a beret in front of the SLA's seven-headed cobra symbol.

General Field Marshal Cinque (Donald DeFreeze) made a demand for food to be distributed to poor people as a "good faith gesture," and Patty Hearst's father complied by creating a program called People in Need. But riots over the food sidelined the poorly organized program, which displeased Patty and her captors.

Patty's parents were sure she was being brainwashed. But when the SLA then demanded $6 million for Patty's release, her father, Randolph Hearst, protested that it was beyond his capabilities. Dismayed that her parents were debating over her worth in dollars and cents, Patty turned against them and declared allegiance to the SLA, saying on a recording: "I have been given the choice of being released . . . or joining the forces of the Symbionese Liberation Army and fighting for my freedom and the freedom of all oppressed people. I have chosen to stay and fight." She announced she was renaming herself "Tania" after a "comrade who fought alongside Che in Bolivia."

Over two months after her abduction, "Tania" and four SLA members were caught on a surveillance camera holding up a branch office of the Hibernia Bank in San Francisco. They got away with $10,000. Now Hearst was wanted by the FBI, not as a kidnapping victim but as a criminal. In another recording, Patty assured listeners of her willing participation in the robbery and referred to her family as the "pig Hearsts."

Then, Patty was involved in another robbery in Los Angeles. While one SLA member attempted to shoplift from a sporting goods store, Patty, sitting in the getaway car, shot twenty-seven bullets into the storefront. The next day, the Los Angeles Police Department tracked down six SLA members in an apartment in Compton, and a gun battle ensued between SWAT teams and the revolutionaries, all of which was aired on live TV. The six members in the house (including DeFreeze) were killed, but Patty Hearst and her accomplices in the latest robbery were safely ensconced in a hotel nearby. When Patty and the remaining SLA members sent the media a recorded eulogy for the murdered members of their group, Randolph Hearst withdrew his offer of $50,000 for his daughter's safe return.

After many more months of robberies and even another murder, the heiress-gone-wild and three other SLA members were finally arrested in San Francisco in September 1975. When asked for her occupation while being booked, Patty Hearst famously told the officer "urban guerrilla." After a sensational trial, Patty was found guilty of armed robbery and sentenced to seven years in prison. She served twenty-two months before having her sentence commuted by President Jimmy Carter. Patty's kidnappers served eight years in prison. The SLA had finally been squashed by the "fascist insect" they had railed against.

# MEMBERSHIP REQUIREMENTS

In the eyes of young radicals in the SLA, black inmates, no matter what their crime, took on heroic proportions as political prisoners, oppressed by a racist and corrupt American society—which made escaped convict Donald DeFreeze an ideal leader. The other SLA members were mostly white, well-educated, upper-class young men and women. They all took new names such as Fahizah, Zoya, Teko, Yolanda, Gelina, Osceola, Bo, Cujo, and Gabi. DeFreeze took the name Cinque from the leader of the 1839 mutiny on the slave ship *Amistad*. But simply embracing revolutionary rhetoric wasn't enough to make a good SLA member—you had to be prepared to take violent action.

## INSIDE THE SLA

Since a liberal arts education doesn't cover handling machine guns, these kids had a few things to learn. Armed with stolen weapons and funded by robberies, the group trained in military maneuvers in the Berkeley hills. They lived together in various safe houses where guns and free and open sex were plentiful.

Patty Hearst says that early in her captivity, she was kept blindfolded in a closet, terrified and forced to have sex with SLA men. One of them was Willie Wolfe, known in the SLA as "Cujo." When he died in the Los Angeles shootout, Patty was mournful in her radio eulogy, saying: "Cujo was the gentlest, most beautiful man I have ever known. Neither Cujo or I had ever loved an individual the way we loved each other . . . I was ripped off by the pigs when they murdered Cujo."

But during her trial, she disavowed this notion. Later, Patty said of Cujo: "He was just as bad as any of the rest of them, and I think it's insulting to anyone who's ever been raped to suggest that that could turn into a seduction and love affair afterward. It's outrageous."

No matter what methods of coercion the SLA may or may not have used, in the end the jury didn't buy Patty's brainwashing defense. She was convicted of bank robbery, and the guilty verdict dominated headlines around the world. ▲

# STOCKHOLM SYNDROME,
# I NEVER WANNA GO HOME

Stockholm syndrome is a psychological condition in which a captive comes to identify and sympathize with the captor. But what's that have to do with the capital of Sweden? The term was coined after the 1973 robbery of Kreditbanken in Stockholm, Sweden. The two robbers held four bank employees hostage for five days in a bank vault, during which time, the victims got very chummy with their captors. They wound up so emotionally attached that they even defended the bad guys after the ordeal.

Stockholm Syndrome tends to develop in situations where a more dominant individual has the power to put the victim's life in danger, yet the victim must also be shown enough kindness to suppress their anger and fear. The perpetrator need not lay it on thick, though—sometimes, simply a lack of abuse and fulfilment of the victim's most basic needs of survival is enough for the victim to concentrate on the perpetrator's "good side." Most criminals fear and resent law enforcement officials, and when this attitude is adopted by a hostage, it is another hallmark of Stockholm Syndrome. This may account for Patty Hearst's allegiance to the SLA, who demonized the police and other authority figures.

Though Stockholm Syndrome often increases a victim's chances of survival, it is not developed voluntarily. As puzzling as it may seem to those who have not experienced it, Stockholm Syndrome is even more baffling to those who have, having been betrayed by their own minds to identify with evil.

# REVOLUTION NOW!

These militant groups were armed and ready to fight for change.

## THE BLACK PANTHER PARTY

Formed in Oakland, California, in 1966, the Black Panthers were a revolutionary party that sought to empower African Americans. They didn't intend to combat racism with sit-ins and messages of peace like some other activists of the time—they made it clear they would defend themselves by force. Members were trained in self-defense tactics and marched in public with weapons displayed, intimidating onlookers with their military precision.

*A Black Panther convention at the Lincoln Memorial, 1970.*

The Panthers had a "Ten-Point Program," a list of goals with a socialist agenda. These included demands for housing and employment, and to have all black men exempt from military service and released from prison. While the Black Panthers may not have won everything they wanted, their well-organized movement spread to many other US cities where there were large populations of African Americans. The Panthers provided these underserved communities with medical care and tutoring, as education was a priority to the movement. They also pulled together to clean up run-down neighborhoods.

Despite their positive contributions, the Black Panthers are remembered today largely for violence. They railed against police brutality and were involved in shoot-outs with law enforcement in California, New York, and Chicago that left several Panthers and police officers dead. By the mid-70s, the party's militant methods had fallen out of favor, and by the early 80s, the group was effectively disbanded.

## THE WEATHER UNDERGROUND

This organization, also known as the Weathermen, was founded on the Ann Arbor campus of the University of Michigan in 1968. In that tumultuous year, civil rights leader Martin Luther King Jr. and liberal Senator Robert Kennedy were assassinated, and protests against the Vietnam War turned violent at the Democratic National Convention in Chicago and Columbia University.

The leftist organization Students for a Democratic Society (SDS) was on the front lines in response to these events, standing in opposition to racism and inequality in America, and to the country's imperialistic machinations overseas. The Weather Underground was a more radical splinter group of SDS that used violence as a means of affecting social and political change. They were named for a line in the Bob Dylan song "Subterranean Homesick Blues" that goes: "You don't need a weatherman to know which way the wind blows"—and for the Weathermen, the winds of change were moving in an ominous direction.

In 1969, two Black Panthers were killed in a Chicago police raid, which many suspected was a government-sanctioned killing. If the government wanted to wipe out militant groups, then the Weathermen would refuse to back down. Instead, they issued a "declaration of war," encouraging America's young people to take up arms and "join forces in the destruction of the empire." The Weathermen planned to enact this destruction by planting bombs at sites such as the US Army base at Fort Dix in New Jersey. But their plan went awry when the pipe bombs they were building in the basement of a New York City townhouse accidentally detonated, killing three people and driving other Weather Underground members into hiding for many years.

But this tragedy wasn't the end of the Weathermen. Before the group disbanded in 1976, they bombed many police precincts and government buildings, including the Pentagon and the United States Capitol. In 1980, reputed leaders of the group Bill Ayers and Bernardine Dohrn turned themselves in and began a new life in Chicago. The consequences of their actions were surprisingly lenient—because it was revealed that the FBI used illegal methods to surveil the Weathermen and other subversive groups, Dohrn ended up having to pay a fine of $1,500 and spend three years on probation. Ayers, who was never convicted of any crime, later became a professor at the University of Chicago.

Ayars's and Dohrn's family lived in the same neighborhood as another notorious family, the Obamas. When Barack Obama ran for president in 2008, Ayers made a small contribution to his campaign. This connection, though tenuous, was problematic for Obama, who was accused of fraternizing with terrorists. Obama denied having a relationship with Ayers and condemned the violent actions of the Weathermen. For the Weather Underground, there was a thin line between activism and terrorism. ▲

*Thugs Strangling a Traveller*

# THUGGEES

FOUNDED: *The first printed reference to Thugs is found in* History of Fīrūz Shāh *(a book of Indian history), by Ziauddin Barani, dated around 1356.*

STATUS: *The Thuggees were eradicated by the British rulers of India by the late 1800s.*

EXCLUSIVITY FACTOR: *High, since membership was most likely hereditary.*

SECRECY FACTOR: *Thuggee bands traveled openly, but didn't let their criminal intentions be known until they infiltrated groups of other travelers and ambushed them under cover of night.*

THREAT FACTOR: *Pretty high, being a band of mass murderers and all.*

QUIRK FACTOR: *Thugs make appearances in many works of film and litera-ture, most notably the 1984 movie* Indiana Jones and the Temple of Doom, *where the arch villain is a Thuggee chieftain.*

## HISTORY AND BACKGROUND

When you hear the word "thug," you probably think of modern urban ruffians—but the term originated centuries ago to describe the gangs of bandits prowling the rural South Asian subcontinent. Woe to the traveler who was waylaid by the Thuggees on India's desolate back roads. These murderous marauders would strangle their victims, purportedly following precise religious rites to honor Kali, the Hindu goddess of destruction. Then they would plunder the bodies and move on.

Thuggees terrorized travelers for hundreds of years, taking thousands of lives. It was not until these dastardly deeds came to the attention of agents of the British East India Company in the 1800s that Thugism began to be suppressed. With cooperation from local municipalities, who also wanted to eliminate the Thugs, British Officer William Sleeman succeeded in capturing over three thousand of the alleged murderers. Over four hundred of them were hanged, and the rest imprisoned or rehabilitated. Sleeman's efforts were honored with an Indian village in his name—Sleemanabad, where his picture still hangs in the police station today.

Sleeman's accounts of the Thugs even inspired a bestselling novel called *Confessions of a Thug*, by Phillip Meadows Taylor. This sensational volume thrilled Victorians fascinated with the exotic culture of the East. Even young Queen Victoria was a fan.

It is important to note, however, that colonial history is written by the victors, and the British campaign against the Thugs might have been a little less than heroic—it has even been likened to a witch hunt. Overzealous enforcers likely captured unrelated bands of nomads and branded them as Thugs. It is said that Sleeman used torture to extract confessions and conducted criminal trials in English, which the accused did not understand. Like the killers he despised, Sleeman, too, had a ruthless side, and hanged Thugs on mango trees over a distance of two hundred and fifty miles as a warning to would-be baddies.

Through these initiatives, the Thug cult was completely abolished by the 1890s, but the notion of criminal castes still survives in India.

# MEMBERSHIP REQUIREMENTS

Thuggees were no lone highwaymen—they were a highly organized band of professional assassins with their own customs, rituals, and language. The Thugs traced their origins to seven Muslim tribes, but Hindus were also associated with them, and they were thought to be united by their worship of Kali (though that detail also may have been exaggerated by their British conquerors, who had no love for Hinduism).

Like many social stations in India at the time, Thuggee status was hereditary, passed from father to son. The Thugs were portrayed in William Sleeman's accounts as loyal and devoted family men—but their family business was a gruesome one.

## INSIDE THE CULT OF THUGGEE

The Thugs allegedly kicked off each of their killing sprees with a ritual devoted to the goddess Kali, who is said to have generously presented them with one of her teeth for a pickaxe, a rib for a knife, and the hem of her lower dress for a noose. The pickaxe, in particular, was of great importance. The tool could only be fabricated in secret, and when finished, had to be consecrated in an elaborate ceremony involving cleansing the axe in sugar water and sour milk, passing it through a fire stoked with cow dung seven times, and then using it to strike a coconut. If the coconut did not split with one blow, conditions were understood to be unfavorable, and the entire ritual had to be conducted all over again on a different day.

But when it was successful, the Thugs were could embark on the hunt for victims. A trustworthy Thug (well, trustworthy for a killer con man) was chosen to transport the sacred pickaxe on the journey. Once in camp, the axe was placed under the protection of the goddess, buried with the tip pointing in the direction the group intended to proceed. If Kali preferred an alternate route, they trusted her to reposition the axe to show them where to go—sort of like a deadly game of spin the bottle.

Next, the Thugs donned disguises—they may have presented themselves as a band of musicians or wealthy merchants. Then, when they came across another band of travelers—one they outnumbered—on a lonely road, they went in for the kill. Following the lead of the charming gang chief, the Thugs persuaded the travelers to let them join their group. Once welcomed by their victims, the Thugs would travel with them for a time, sometimes several days, gaining their confidence and friendship. Then, when their victims were least expecting it, they would strike.

A nighttime gathering around the fire could easily turn into a massacre with the Thugs in camp. When it came time to kill, their patience turned to pitilessness. The chief would give them a signal, often a commonplace remark like "Bring the tobacco." Then, the stranglers would throw scarves around the victims' necks and garrote them, while other Thugs held down the victims' arms. The bodies were stripped of all identification, cut open, and thrown into graves. The Thugs would then abscond into the night with their possessions. The operation was quick and efficient.

Often, the plunder didn't amount to much, but the clever Thugs sometimes managed to get other perks from their victims. Mark Twain tells of a gang of Thugs who "fell in with a couple of barbers and persuaded them to come along in their company by promising them the job of shaving the whole crew—thirty Thugs. At the place appointed for the murder fifteen got shaved, and actually paid the barbers for their work. Then killed them and took back the money."

Women, children, and people of certain castes were sometimes spared by the Thugs, but not always. If the omens indicated that they had Kali's blessing, rumor had it that the Thugs would feel no remorse for what they had done. ▲

# GANGSTER'S PARADISE

Great American author Mark Twain was familiar with environs far beyond the banks of the Mississippi River. In his travelogue *Following the Equator*, he helps explain why the Thuggees got away with murder for so long.

*It was the division of the country into so many States and nations that made Thuggee possible and prosperous. It is difficult to realize the situation. But perhaps one may approximate it by imagining the States of our Union peopled by separate nations, speaking separate languages, with guards and custom-houses strung along all frontiers, plenty of interruptions for travelers and traders, interpreters able to handle all the languages very rare or non-existent, and a few wars always going on here and there and yonder. . . . It would make intercommunication in a measure ungeneral. India had eighty languages, and more custom-houses than cats. No clever man with the instinct of a highway robber could fail to notice what a chance for business was here offered. . . and so, quite naturally, the brotherhood of the Thugs came into being. . . .*

*There were no public conveyances. There were no conveyances for hire. The traveler went on foot or in a bullock cart or on a horse. . . . As soon as he was out of his own little State or principality he was among strangers; nobody knew him, nobody took note of him, and from that time his movements could no longer be traced. . . . Whenever he was between villages he was an easy prey, particularly as he usually traveled by night, to avoid the heat. He was always being overtaken by strangers who offered him the protection of their company, or asked for the protection of his—and these strangers were often Thugs, as he presently found out to his cost. The landholders, the native police, the petty princes, the village officials, the customs officers were in many cases protectors and harborers of the Thugs, and betrayed travelers to them for a share of the spoil. . . .*

Dressed to kill.

All through a vast continent, thus infested, helpless people of every
caste and kind moved along the paths and trails silently by night,

JULIE TIBBOTT IS AN EDITOR OF TEEN FICTION AT A

MAJOR PUBLISHING HOUSE. SHE LIVES ON NEW YORK

CITY'S LOWER EAST SIDE, ONCE HOME TO MANY ORGANIZED

CRIME SYNDICATES, STREET

GANGS, AND UNDERGROUND ANAR-

CHISTS. SHE'S NOT A MEMBER OF

ANY SECRET SOCIETIES. ___ OR

IS SHE?